Words of Wisdom

"The tragedy of life is what dies inside a man while he lives."

Albert Einstein

"Love is the only gold."

Alfred, Lord Tennyson

"Cover for me!"

Homer Simpson

"A good listener is usually thinking of something else."

Kin Hubbard

"Dogs look up to you. Cats look down on you. Pigs treat you as equal."

Winston Churchill

"The easiest thing in the world is to tell the truth. Then you don't have to remember what you said."

Robert Evans

"History repeats itself as farce."

Karl Marx

"Irony is the hygiene of the mind."

Elizabeth Bibesco

"Fools rush in where fools have been before."

Unknown

"I only drink to steady my nerves. Sometimes I'm so steady I don't move for months."

W.C. Fields

"A hard man is good to find."

Mae West

Words of Wisdom

From the greatest minds of all time

Mick Farren

Chrysalis

First published in the United States in 2004 by
Chrysalis
The Chrysalis Building
Bramley Road, London, W10 6SP
An imprint of **Chrysalis** Books Group

Text © Mick Farren 2004

Volume © Chrysalis Books Group plc 2004

Library of Congress Control Number:
A catalog record for this book is available from the Library of Congress.

1 2 3 4 5 6 7 8 9 10

ISBN: 0-681-04864-6

Designed by Philip Clucas MSIAD
Printed and bound in Malaysia

Contents

Introduction:
Words of the Wise and the Sages of the Ages

It is a good thing for an uneducated man to read books of quotations.

Winston Churchill

Quotation is a serviceable substitute for wit.

Oscar Wilde

Cover for me!

Homer Simpson

As we travel through what is laughingly called life, one of the things that becomes increasingly and indisputably obvious is that we need all the help we can get. Some may turn to soothsayers, or TV talk shows, and others to a religion of their choice. Some may read their horoscopes or talk to their psychiatrists. Friends and bartenders, and even strangers on a train or plane, are taken at their word as we attempt to get to grips with the problems, and solve the puzzles, that life throws at us in an unrelenting stream. Here in the 21st century, we are forced to cope with corporations, and contend with computers. A simple phone call comes with unbelievably complex options. One can be arrested for making jokes at airports, and to talk to a bank teller requires three different kinds of identification. As the walls of our so-called civilisation close in on us, where are we going to turn to for advanced wisdom in this modern world? Who we gonna call?

Once upon a time, a wealth of folk wisdom was contained within the extended family, but amid the mobile, cellular, transitory and high rise, the family has become so fragmented that such resources are all but gone. Many of us increasingly look to our culture and the media for directions, tips and pointers, but how heavily can we rely on a media or consumer culture that inevitably wants to sell us something? The classics of art and literature almost by definition can be trusted, but how many of us can truthfully say that we have read even a fraction of all the great books, or seen anything like all the great plays and films, or listened to the full sweep of great music?

In this era of high-speed communication, we all need short cuts, hot-links, easy access. We need these things condensed, reduced to the essence. We simply do not have time to browse and digest. We cannot possibly sit down and read the entire works of the philosopher Friedrich Nietzsche. The phone would ring, the Prozac would wear off, someone would urgently need our undivided attention, or there would be something appealing on television. We would close the book before even consuming a fraction of the thoughts of Ol' Friedrich. But, then again, why should we bother? All most of us need to know about Nietzsche is that he coined a few handy phrases, the most famous of which is the ever popular, "That which does not kill us makes us stronger". The same applies to Oscar Wilde and Albert Einstein, to Virgil and Hunter S. Thompson. Some of us may actually have watched every episode of *The Simpsons*, but how many of us have total recall of every one of Homer's insights?

But now you don't need to search alone. *Words of Wisdom*, casting the widest and most ecumenical net, has done it all for you. The first quote is on money by Tennessee Williams, and the last words to live by are from Jeff Spicolli. In between are nearly 2000 razor-sharp comments, obsessively collected and culled over a period of years, that include observations by everyone from Elvis Presley to Galileo, from Groucho Marx to Tony Soprano. For the reader it's no fuss, no muss, and very little effort. All the wisdom of the sages of the ages in one handy, biodegradable volume; read them, ruminate on them, remember them...and then quote them to impress. One can never be too rich or too thin – or too witty or too erudite.

Mick Farren, Los Angeles, 2004

" Words on Money "

The root of all evil, the key to all doors, the constant preoccupation, and don't forget, crime doesn't pay (so they say)...

You can be young without money, but you can't be old without it.

Tennessee Williams

I'm not interested in money. I just want to be wonderful.

Marilyn Monroe

The amount of money one needs is terrifying.

Ludwig van Beethoven

I feel closest to Hell when I'm thinking about money.

Pharaoh Sanders

I rob banks because that's where the money is.

Willie Sutton

Money talks...but all mine ever says is good-bye.

Anon

Money is like manure. You have to spread it around or it smells.

J. Paul Getty

In its famous paradox, the equation of money and
excrement, psychoanalysis becomes the first science
to state what common sense and the poets have long known –
that the essence of money is in its absolute worthlessness.

Norman O. Brown

The entire essence of America is the hope to first make
money – then make money with money – then make lots
of money with lots of money.

Paul Erdman

Buy land. They ain't making any more of the stuff.

Will Rogers

The buck stops with the guy who signs the checks.

Rupert Murdoch

Sudden money is going from zero to two hundred dollars a week.
The rest doesn't count.

Neil Simon

Money is the barometer of a society's virtue.

Ayn Rand

Finance is the art of passing currency from hand to hand
until it finally disappears.

Robert W. Sarnoff

Money is the most egalitarian force in society. It confers
power on whoever holds it.

Roger Starr

Money may kindle, but it cannot by itself,
and for very long, burn.

Igor Stravinski

Money is the last refuge of people who have been scared by life.

John Cassavetes

Money is better than poverty, if only for financial reasons.

Woody Allen

Money costs too much.

Ross McDonald

Money has no smell.

Emperor Vespasian

Gimme my money, and I'll get the hell out.

Elvis Presley

I don't mind being ripped off as long as I'm told
I'm being ripped off.

Steve Peregrin Took

To my knowledge, no model projecting directional movements
in exchange rates is as good as flipping a coin.

Alan Greenspan

There are two things that are important in politics. The first is
money and I can't remember what the second one is.

Mark Hanna

I should have been a plumber. Plumbers get paid.

Noel Redding

A little bit of inflation is good for you.

The Economist

Capitalism needs to function like a game of tug-of-war.
Two opposing sides need to continually struggle for
dominance, but at no time can either side be permitted
to walk away with the rope.

Pete Holiday

Borrow money from pessimists: they don't expect it back.

Steven Wright

Those with the gold make the rules.

Jack Osbourne

The dynamics of capitalism is postponement of enjoyment
to the constantly postponed future.

Norman O. Brown

Greed, for want of a better word, is good.

Gordon Gecko

Only a poor man and a blind man can play,
and if you're poor, step away.

Big Kate

Money is fantastic. It's the best thing in the world.

Simon Cowell

Let me tell you something about the very rich.
They are different to you and me.

F. Scott Fitzgerald

Every crowd has a silver lining.

P. T. Barnum

So you think that money is the root of all evil.
Have you ever asked what is the root of all money?

Ayn Rand

Ninety percent of my salary I spent on booze and women –
the rest I wasted.

Tug McGraw

In the affluent society no useful distinction can be made
between luxuries and necessaries.

J. K. Galbraith

The avoidance of taxes is the only intellectual pursuit that
carries any reward.

John Maynard Keynes

Money can change people's minds about most things.

Charlie Daniels

Money doesn't make you happy. I now have $50 million,
but I was just as happy when I had $48 million.

Arnold Schwarzenegger

Money will not make you happy,
and happy will not make you money.

Groucho Marx

17

After money in the bank, a grudge is the next best thing.

Anthony Trollope

There are only two kinds of money in the world:
your money and my money.

Milton Friedman

Eat the rich, yum, yum.

Left-wing catchphrase

A fool and his money are lucky to meet in the first place.

W.C. Fields

Having all that money doesn't mean much
if it's just sitting there.

Angelina Jolie

A bank is a place to lend you money if you can prove
that you don't need it.

Bob Hope

Do not ask for credit as a refusal may offend.

Sign in liquor store

Money talks, bullshit walks.

Various attributions

If you own the property you're a king.
Otherwise you're a peon.

Robert Evans

Property is theft.

Leftist slogan

Follow the money.
> *Deep Throat's instruction to Bob Woodward and Carl Bernstein*

The two most beautiful words in the English language
are "check enclosed".

Dorothy Parker

What's money? A man is a success if he gets up in
the morning and goes to bed at night and in between
does what he wants to do.

Bob Dylan

I renounce my art to make money,
and then make no money.

Dylan Thomas

You can't afford me.

Keith Moon

19

Words on Love

It makes the world go around, love hurts, it's a many splendoured thing, you know it can't be bad...

Love conquers all.

Virgil

Love your enemies.

Jesus of Nazareth

Love is the only gold.

Alfred, Lord Tennyson

Who, being loved, is poor?

Oscar Wilde

One can't be rhapsodically in love all the time,
because when would one shave?

Lord Byron

Love does not consist of gazing at each other, but looking
in the same direction.

Antoine de Saint-Exupery

Dignity and love do not blend well, nor do they continue
long together.

Ovid

Love is the flower of life, and blossoms unexpectedly
and without law, and must be plucked before it is found,
and enjoyed for the brief hour of its duration.

D.H. Lawrence

Desire makes everything blossom; possession makes
everything wither and fade.

Marcel Proust

Only time can heal your broken heart, just as only time
can heal his broken arms and legs.

Miss Piggy

Self love is the least fickle variety.

Oscar Wilde

Who loves believes the impossible.

Elizabeth Barrett Browning

Many a man has fallen in love with a girl in a light so dim
he would not have chosen a suit by it.

Maurice Chevalier

It is impossible not to love someone who makes toast for you.

Nigel Slater

To see you naked is to recall the Earth.

Frederico Garcia Lorca

People should mate for life, like pigeons or Catholics.

Woody Allen

Love is a fire. But whether it is going to warm your heart
or burn down your house, you can never tell.

Joan Crawford

Passion, I see, is catching.

William Shakespeare

It is useless to hold a person to anything he says while
he's in love, drunk, or running for office.

Shirley MacLaine

What the world really needs is more love and less paperwork.

Pearl Bailey

A true revolutionary is guided by a great feeling of love.

Che Guevara

The light that lies in women's eyes has been my heart's undoing.

Thomas Moore

The reduction of the universe to a single being, the
expansion of a single being even to God, this is love.

Victor Hugo

Gravitation can not be held responsible for people falling in love.

Albert Einstein

Love is the only sane and satisfactory answer to the
problem of human existence.

Erich Fromm

True love is like seeing ghosts; we all talk about it,
but few of us have ever seen one.

Rochefoucauld

Faults are thick where love is thin.

English proverb

Nothing spoils the taste of peanut butter like unrequited love.

Charlie Brown

People think that love is an emotion. Love is good sense.

Ken Kesey

One word frees us of all the weight and pain in life.
That word is love.

Sophocles

The first duty of love is to listen.

Paul Tillich

Any time not spent on love is wasted.

Torquato Tasso

The only thing we never get enough of is love;
and the only thing we never give enough of is love.

Henry Miller

Love is a great beautifier.

Louisa May Alcott

Love is the delightful interval between meeting a beautiful girl
and discovering she looks like a haddock.

John Barrymore

The heart has reasons that reason does not understand.

Blaise Pascal

In our life there is a single color, as on an artist's palette,
which provides the meaning of life and art.
It is the color of love.

Marc Chagall

Do you love me because I am beautiful, or am I beautiful
because you love me?

Cinderella

Age does not protect you from love. But love, to some extent,
protects you from age.

Jeanne Moreau

Love is an ideal thing, marriage a real thing; a confusion
of the real with the ideal never goes unpunished.

Goethe

A man falls in love through his eyes, a woman through her ears.

Woodrow Wyatt

I like not only to be loved, but to be told that I am loved.

George Eliot

True love casts out fear. If you're afraid of me then there's
something wrong with you.

Charles Manson

Love: The irresistible desire to be irresistibly desired.

Robert Frost

Love is a canvas furnished by Nature and embroidered
by imagination.

Voltaire

At the touch of love, everyone becomes a poet.

Plato

It takes a love story to cure love.

Porthos the Musketeer

Some of us think holding on makes us strong;
but sometimes it is letting go.

Herman Hesse

We'll always have Paris.

Rick Blaine

Frankly, my dear, I don't give a damn.

Rhett Butler

" Words about Sex "

The average human being supposedly thinks about sex at least once every fourteen minutes...

Take your pleasure where you can.

Julian Kaye

Love is the answer, but while you're waiting for the answer, sex raises some pretty good questions.

Woody Allen

Casual sex is a f**king good thing.

Colin Farrell

If she's beautiful, it's hard to say no.

Steve McQueen

Orgasms don't last long enough.

Courtney Cox

Women need a reason to have sex – men just need a place.

Billy Crystal

Never play cards with a man named Doc, never eat at a place
called Mom's, never sleep with anyone whose problems are
worse than your own.

Nelson Algren

Commit adultery with people who have as much to lose
as you do.

Adage

If it weren't for pickpockets I'd have no sex life at all.

Rodney Dangerfield

Men don't pay prostitutes for sex.
They pay them to leave afterwards.

Germaine Greer

You know why blondes have more fun?
They're easier to find in the dark.

Dolly Parton

Exciting things tend to happen when you wear a skirt slit
to your waist.

Louis Chunn

Pleasure's a sin and sometimes sin's a pleasure.

Lord Byron

No one ever suddenly became depraved.

Juvenal

There is nothing wrong with going to bed with someone
of your own sex. People should be very free with sex, they
should draw the line at goats.

Elton John

I don't mind where people make love so long as they don't do it
in the street and frighten the horses.

Mrs. Patrick Campbell

Power is the ultimate aphrodisiac.

Henry Kissinger

No girl was ever seduced by a book.

Jimmy Walker

Brevity is the soul of lingerie.

Dorothy Parker

I dress for women, and undress for men.

Angie Dickinson

I want to f**k Angie Dickinson. Let's see who gets lucky first.

Corrado Soprano

Be sure to wear a good cologne, a nice aftershave lotion,
and a strong underarm deodorant. And it might be a good idea
to wear some clothes, too.

George Burns

Sex is the most compressed set of circumstances that we've got.
Everything is in that collision.

Arthur Miller

When you are said to be the best f**k of the century,
it's a matter of course that every woman is disappointed
after the first night.

Mick Jagger

Mick's infidelity used to exhaust all my energy.

Jerry Hall

Sex is the most awful filthy thing on earth and you should
save it for someone you love.

Buck Hancock

Sex is boring.

Sid Vicious

And if a woman shall approach unto any beast, and lie down
thereto, thou shalt kill the woman and the beast.

Leviticus 20:16

There she lusted after her lovers whose genitals were like those
of donkeys and whose emissions were like those of horses.

Ezekiel 23:20

I tried phone sex – it gave me an ear infection.

Richard Lewis

Being a sex symbol is a heavy load to carry,
especially when one is tired, hurt and bewildered.

Marilyn Monroe

Sex appeal is 50 per cent what you've got and 50 per cent
what people think you've got.

Sophia Loren

It's been so long since I made love I can't even remember who
gets tied up.

Joan Rivers

I advocate the bringing back of the birch but only for consenting
adults.

Gore Vidal

'Tis the season to be vile.

Graham Norton

There's nothing better than good sex. But bad sex?
A peanut butter and jelly sandwich is better than bad sex.

Billy Joel

Any idiot can get laid when they're famous.
That's easy. It's getting laid when you're not famous
that takes some talent.

Kevin Bacon

At least she's the one holding the whip.

Patsy Stone

There is nothing safe about sex. There never will be.

Norman Mailer

The first time I had sex I was so frightened.
I mean, I was all alone.

Rodney Dangerfield

I've tried several varieties of sex. The conventional position
makes me claustrophobic and the others give me a stiff neck
or lockjaw.

Tallulah Bankhead

Pursuit and seduction are the essence of sexuality.
It's part of the sizzle.

Camille Paglia

A hard man is good to find.

Mae West

A man can sleep around, no questions asked, but if a woman
makes nineteen or twenty mistakes she's a tramp.

Joan Rivers

In America sex is an obsession, in other parts of the world
it is a fact.

Marlene Dietrich

One thing I've learned in all these years is not to make love
when you really don't feel it; there's probably nothing worse
you can do to yourself than that.

Norman Mailer

I wanted sex to be like robbing life out of the jaws of death!

Robin Green

Sex is God's joke on human beings.

Bette Davis

Words on Women and Men

Incompatible, often at war, can't live with them, and yet can't understand them...

A woman of the world doesn't have friends –
she has lovers and acquaintances.

John Galsworthy

Happiness is the sublime moment when you get out
of your corsets.

Edith Wharton

Suffer a woman not to usurp authority over man, but to be in
silence.

1 Timothy 2:12

The women come to see the show, they come to make a show
themselves.

Ovid

Women with degrees are 50% less likely to become mothers.

Statistic

Sometimes being a bitch is all a woman has to hold on to.

Dolores Claiborne

People call me a feminist whenever I express sentiments
that differentiate me from a doormat or a prostitute.

Rebecca West

If I hadn't been a woman, I'd have been a drag queen.

Dolly Parton

Girls are psycho.

Jenna Jameson

Seek a woman who has no aspirations to be an actress
and is therefore from this planet.

James Woods

Women, as our parents did not teach us, prefer bastards.

Jeremy Grady

Just standing around looking beautiful is so boring,
really boring, so boring.

Michelle Pfeiffer

Girls are more bendy than boys.

Eddie Izzard

There are three things men can do with women: love them, suffer for them, or turn them into literature.

Stephen Stills

Last week I saw a woman flayed, and you will hardly believe how much it altered her person for the worse.

Jonathan Swift

You can forget a lot of things, but you cannot forget a woman's name and claim to love her.

Real Live Preacher

The definition of a beautiful woman is one who loves me.

Sloan Wilson

The world is controlled by seven women.

John Cassavetes

For a man's work you need a man's outfit.

Catherine the Great

No woman, no crime.

Jimmy the Doorman

The modern rule is that every woman should be her
own chaperon.

Amy Vanderbilt

No woman ever lacked elegance because of an excess of
simplicity.

Genevieve Dariaux

Don't accept rides from strange men, and remember
that all men are strange.

Robin Morgan

Scratch an actor and you will find an actress.

Sophia Myles

Scratch a successful female and you will find a father.

Stella McCartney

Women upset everything. When you let them into your life,
you find that the woman is driving at one thing and you're
driving at another.

George Bernard Shaw

Misogynist: A man who hates women as much as women
hate one another.

H.L. Mencken

I hate women because they always know where things are.

James Thurber

What is most beautiful in virile men is something feminine; what is most beautiful in feminine women is something masculine.

Susan Sontag

Women who seek to be equal with men lack ambition.

Timothy Leary

For most of history, Anonymous was a woman.

Virginia Woolf

Men are like a deck of cards. You'll find the occasional king, but most are jacks.

Laura Swenson

Men always want to be a woman's first love – women like to be a man's last romance.

Oscar Wilde

The fastest way to a man's heart is through his chest.

Roseanne Barr

A woman needs a man like a fish needs a bicycle.

Feminist graffiti

God gave us a penis and a brain, but only enough blood
to run one at a time.

Robin Williams

I require three things in a man: He must be handsome,
ruthless, and stupid.

Dorothy Parker

The male is a domestic animal which, if treated with firmness,
can be trained to do most things.

Jilly Cooper

I would cease to be a man if I didn't like women.

Che Guevara

Men should either be treated generously or destroyed.

Machiavelli

It's a shame when a man is in prison because of a woman.

Mexican prison guard

Males are, in many ways, parasites upon their partners.

Steve Jones

Boys Are Stupid.

T-shirt slogan

If you want to say it with flowers, a single rose says:
"I'm cheap!"

Delta Burke

Behind every great man there stands an astonished woman.

Lester Pearson

You'd better start showing me a little more respect round here,
Mr. Man.

Annie Wilks

Man is evil, capable of nothing but destruction.

Dr. Zaius

Man is nature's sole mistake.

W.S. Gilbert

Men willingly believe what they wish.

Julius Caesar

All the men I've ever spoken to say they like girls
to have an arse on them.

Kate Winslet

If it has tires or testicles, you're going to have trouble with it.

Linda Furney

If you never want to see a man again, say, "I love you.
I want to marry you. I want to have children" – they leave
skid marks.

Rita Rudner

What really flatters a man is that you think him
worth flattering.

George Bernard Shaw

I'm just a person trapped inside a woman's body.

Elaine Boosler

No man succeeds without a good woman behind
him. Wife or mother, if it is both, he is twice
blessed indeed.

Harold MacMillan

I've never yet met a man who could look after me.
I don't need a husband. What I need is a wife.

Joan Collins

As far as I am concerned, being any gender is a drag.

Patti Smith

" Words on Friendship "

The one on whom you can depend until the end, but with friends like these, who needs enemies...?

A friend in need is a pest, get rid of him.

Tommy Cooper

It's the friends you can call up at four a.m. that matter.

Marlene Dietrich

I would rather have an intelligent enemy than a stupid friend.

Diego Alphonso Equanja

You can make new friends, but you can't make old friends.

Martin Amis

I always like to know everything about my new friends,
and nothing about my old ones.

Oscar Wilde

Strangers are just friends you don't yet fear, resent,
or compete with.

Victoria Coren

It's better to have a known enemy than a forced ally.

Napoleon Bonaparte

Have no friends not equal to yourself.

Confucius

Before borrowing money from a friend,
decide which you need the most.

American proverb

Keep your friends close, but your enemies closer.

Vito Corleone

Faithless is he that says farewell when the road darkens.

J.R.R. Tolkien

There's only two people I trust. One of them's me
and the other's not you.

Cameron Poe

A friend's eye is a good mirror.

Old Irish proverb

Friendship is the hardest thing in the world to explain. It's not something you learn in school. But if you haven't learned the meaning of friendship, you really haven't learned anything.

Muhammad Ali

Friends are treasures.

Horace Burns

An insincere and evil friend is more to be feared than a wild beast; a wild beast may wound your body, but an evil friend will wound your mind.

Buddha

The only way to have a friend is to be one.

Ralph Waldo Emerson

A friend is one who knows you and loves you just the same.

Elbert Hubbard

Like great statesmen, we encourage those who betray their friends.

John Gay

Misfortune shows those who are not really friends.

Aristotle

A good friend can tell you what is the matter with you in a minute. He may not seem such a good friend after telling.

Arthur Brisbane

The meeting of two personalities is like the contact of two chemical substances: if there is any reaction, both are transformed.

Carl Jung

Money can't buy you friends, but you get a better class of enemies.

Spike Milligan

Never keep up with the Joneses. Drag them down to your level.

Quentin Crisp

My mother used to say that there are no strangers, only friends you haven't met yet. She's now in a maximum security twilight home in Australia.

Dame Edna Everage

True friends stab you in the front.

Oscar Wilde

With friends like these, who needs enemies?

Various attributions

Never explain – your friends do not need it and your enemies
will not believe you anyway.

Elbert Hubbard

Nothing changes your opinion of a friend so surely
as success – yours or his.

Franklin P. Jones

It is in the character of very few men to honour
without envy a friend who has prospered.

Aeschylus

When the character of a man is not clear to you,
look at his friends.

Japanese proverb

Reveal not every secret you have to a friend,
for how can you tell but that friend may hereafter
become an enemy.

Saadi

" Words on Marriage "

Two people and an institution, until death do them part, forsaking all others, at least that's the theory...

Marriage is too interesting an experiment to be tried only once.

Eva Gabor

All marriages are happy. It's trying to live together afterwards that causes problems.

Shelley Winters

Bigamy is having one wife too many. Monogamy is the same.

Oscar Wilde

Monogamy is impossible among interesting people.

Erica Jong

The critical period in matrimony is breakfast time.

A.P. Herbert

When I meet a man I ask myself, "Is this the man I want
my children to spend their weekends with?"

Rita Rudner

Marriage is a beautiful thing,
but it's also a battle for moral superiority.

Lisa Simpson

Never go to bed mad. Stay up and fight.

Phyllis Diller

You make the beds, do the dishes, and six months later
you have to start all over again.

Joan Rivers

Can you imagine anything more absurd than
announcing you intend to divorce a woman
who had just fallen into a coma?

Klaus von Bulow

You can't stay married in a situation where you are afraid
to go to sleep in case your wife might cut your throat.

Mike Tyson

Marriage is the wastepaper basket of emotion.

Sidney Webb

I've had diseases that lasted longer than my marriages.

Nell Carter

Marriage is for a little while, but alimony is forever.

Quentin Crisp

I think every woman is entitled to a middle husband
she can forget.

Adela Rogers St. John

You can marry drunk and you can't marry gay?

Whoopi Goldberg

The conception of two people living together for twenty-five
years without having a cross word suggests a lack of spirit
only to be admired in sheep.

Alan Patrick Herbert

All married couples should learn the art of battle
as they should learn the art of making love.

Ann Landers

A simple enough pleasure, surely, to have breakfast
alone with one's husband, but how seldom married people
in the midst of life achieve it.

Anne Morrow Lindbergh

49

All marriages are mixed marriages.

Chantal Saperstein

Happiness just wasn't part of the job description back then. You tried to find a helpmate to keep the cold wind and dogs at bay. Happiness just wasn't part of the equation. Survival was.

Robin Green

There's only one way to have a happy marriage
and as soon as I learn what it is I'll get married again.

Clint Eastwood

I tended to place my wife under a pedestal.

Woody Allen

Marriage is a great institution, but I'm not ready
for an institution yet.

Mae West

Always get married early in the morning. That way,
if it doesn't work out, you haven't wasted a whole day.

Mickey Rooney

In Hollywood a marriage is a success if it outlasts milk.

Rita Rudner

We were happily married for eight months. Unfortunately, we were married for four and a half years.

Nick Faldo

I love being married. It's so great to find that one special person you want to annoy for the rest of your life.

Rita Rudner

My toughest fight was with my first wife.

Muhammad Ali

I'm not a real movie star. I've still got the same wife I started out with twenty-eight years ago.

Will Rogers

By all means marry; if you get a good wife, you'll be happy. If you get a bad one, you'll become a philosopher.

Socrates

Marriage is the only adventure open to the cowardly.

Voltaire

If you want to sacrifice the admiration of many men for the criticism of one, go ahead, get married.

Katharine Hepburn

My ex-wife is writing a book about our marriage. It's
very depressing.

Isaac David

Marriage is an institution, but who wants to live in
an institution.

Groucho Marx (and other attributions)

Marriage is popular because it combines the maximum of
temptation with the maximum of opportunity.

George Bernard Shaw

Few things are more fundamentally reassuring than an up close
and personal look at another couple's unhappiness.

Zoe Heller

I know nothing about sex because I was always married.

Zsa Zsa Gabor

" Words about the Family "

Relatives are relatives, and you are given very little choice in the matter...

Fredo, you're my older brother...and I love you...but don't ever take sides, with anyone, against the family again. Ever.

Michael Corleone

Stone the disobedient children.

Deuteronomy 21:18-21

Happy is said to be the family which can eat onions together. They are, for the time being, separate from the world, and have a harmony of aspiration.

Charles Dudley Warner

A family is a unit composed not only of children but of men, women, an occasional animal, and the common cold.

Ogden Nash

You side with your brother against you cousin, and with your cousin against the foreigners.

Old Arab saying

And Abraham stretched forth his hand,
and took the knife to slay his son.

Genesis 23:10

A man may not marry his mother.

The Book of Common Prayer

I have a sentimental weakness for my children and I spoil them as you can see. They talk when they should listen.

Don Vito Corleone

Childhood is becoming shorter and shorter;
soon it will only last a couple of weekends.

D.J. Enright

Happy families are all alike. Unhappy families are all unhappy in their own way.

Leo Tolstoy

Happy shall be he that taketh and dasheth thy little ones against the stones.

Psalm 137:9

All children are essentially criminal.

Dennis Diderot

You should turn around and face your children
and start following them and listening to them.

Charles Manson

Never have children, only grandchildren.

Gore Vidal

A father is only as happy as his saddest child.

Quincy Jones

God could not be everywhere and therefore he made mothers.

Anon

My mother made me a homosexual.

Graffiti on toilet wall

If I gave her the wool, could she make me one?

Next graffiti on the same wall.

The most remarkable thing about my mother is that for thirty
years she served the family nothing but leftovers. The original
meal has never been found.

Calvin Trillin

Even Attila the Hun had a mother.

Edward Dodd

Being with children is like hanging out with miniature drunks.

Johnny Depp

Ask your child what he wants for dinner only if he's buying.

Fran Lebowitz

Be nice to your children, for they will choose your rest home.

Phyllis Diller

You will never see that miserable brat again.

Charlotte Haze

Happiness is having a large, loving, caring, close-knit
family in another city.

George Burns

If you do that again, mother, I'll have to put you back
in the root cellar.

Norman Bates

If you cannot get rid of the family skeleton
you may as well make him dance.

George Bernard Shaw

Alligators have the right idea, they eat their young.

Mildred Pierce

Get your brother in the band.
Punch his head every now and then.

Noel Gallagher

The place of the father in the modern suburban family
is a very small one, particularly if he plays golf.

Bertrand Russell

My parents only had one argument in forty-five years.
It lasted forty-three years.

Cathy Ladman

By the time a man realizes that maybe his father was right,
he usually has a son who thinks he's wrong.

Charles Wadsworth

The first half of our lives is ruined by our parents,
and the second half by our children.

Clarence Darrow

If your parents never had children,
chances are you won't, either.

Dick Cavett

The gods visit the sins of the fathers upon the children.

Euripides

For rarely are sons similar to their fathers: most are worse,
and a few are better than their fathers.

Homer

The thing that impresses me the most about America
is the way parents obey their children.

King Edward VIII

My mother had a great deal of trouble with me,
but I think she enjoyed it.

Mark Twain

Parents were invented to make children happy by giving them
something to ignore.

Ogden Nash

My father hated radio and could not wait for television to be
invented so he could hate that too.

Peter De Vries

Neurotics build castles in the air, psychotics live in them.
My mother cleans them.

Rita Rudner

The reason grandparents and grandchildren get along
so well is that they have a common enemy.

Sam Levenson

It is a wise father that knows his own child.

William Shakespeare

Some men just aren't cut out for paternity.
Better they should realize it before and not after
they become responsible for a son.

Lois McMaster Bujold

Sooner or later we all quote our mothers.

Bern Williams

Words on Strategy
and Tactics

Be harmless as doves, and as wise as serpents, or dispense with being a dove altogether and flatten the opposition...

Know your enemy and know yourself and you can fight a hundred battles without disaster.

Sun Tzu

Damn the torpedoes, full steam ahead.

David Glasgow Farragut

The first man to raise a fist is the man who has run out of ideas.

H.G. Wells

The first blow is half the battle.

Oliver Goldsmith

The end move in politics is always to pick up a gun.

Buckminster Fuller

Always allow your opponents the opportunity to walk away from the table with dignity because tomorrow they might be your friends.

Mayor Willie Brown

The first thing to decide before you walk into any negotiation is what to do if the other chap says no.

Ernest Bevin

Don't tell people how to do something. Tell them what to do and let them surprise you with their ingenuity.

General George Patton

Don't shoot the apple off your head. Shoot the apple first, and then put it on your head.

Red Bull commercial

Those who would take over the earth and shape it to their will never, I notice, succeed.

Lao Tzu

First attack the heart!

The Green Goblin

Vulcanize the country.

George W. Bush

The ends must justify the means.

Matthew Prior

Use those God-given assets.

Donald Trump

If you want to keep a secret don't tell the boss.

Officer James Malone

Do you have a flag?

Eddie Izzard

Formalities aren't important.

Fidel Castro

Duty largely consists of pretending that the trivial is critical.

John Fowles

Never stop fighting until the fight is won.

Elliot Ness

If you know a better hole go to it.

World War I saying

Beware of the Hun in the sun.

World War I saying (Royal Flying Corps)

If at first you don't succeed, try, try again. Then give up.
No use being a damned fool about it.

W.C. Fields

If, at first, you don't succeed, try, try, try again.
Then use a stunt double.

Arnold Schwarzenegger

If at first you don't succeed, remove all evidence that you tried.

David Brent

Fight downhill.

Sun Tzu

If it's him or you, send flowers.

Nathan Muir

You have to be 100% behind someone before you stab
them in the back.

Ricky Gervais

Fortune favors the bold.

Virgil

Fear is the mind killer.

Bene Geserit maxim

If you don't violate a prisoner's rights some of the time,
then you are not doing your job.

Anonymous CIA official

If a subject refuses to comply after a threat is made, it must
be carried out. If it is not carried out, then other threats become
meaningless.

CIA Interrogation Manual

Honesty may be the best policy, but it's important to
remember that apparently, by elimination, dishonesty
is the second-best policy.

George Carlin

Battles are dangerous affairs.

Wang Hsi

Just juggle the casualty figures.

William S. Burroughs

What I say is, patience, and shuffle the cards.

Miguel de Cervantes

Politics is not the art of the possible. It consists of choosing
between the disastrous and the unpalatable.

John F. Kennedy

Tell him, "I'm in the Mafia and I'll have you killed".

Artie Lang

Use your wit like a foil.

Lord Alfred Douglas

Go after a man's weakness, and never, ever threaten unless you're going to follow through, because if you don't, the next time you won't be taken seriously.

Roy M. Cohn

Release the dogs.

C. Montgomery Burns

If the comrade fails to see your point,
acquaint his face with the pavement.

Leon Trotsky

If you can't beat them, arrange to have them beaten.

George Carlin

When in doubt, bore.

Texan adage

If you can't convince them, confuse them.

Harry S. Truman

If you can't be kind, at least be vague.

Judith Manners

Be more than you seem.

Frederick the Great

Take the bitter with the better.

Conrad Brean

No prisoners!

T.E. Lawrence (of Arabia)

Float like a butterfly, sting like a bee.

Muhammad Ali

Two mice fall in a jug of cream. One drowns, but the other keeps swimming round and round until he has butter and then he staggers away.

Frank Abagnale

A desperate disease requires a dangerous remedy.

Guy Fawkes

Crush your enemies, see them driven before you,
hear the lamentations of their women.

Conan the Barbarian

Nuke the entire site from orbit.

Lieutenant Ripley

When you have done a fault, be always pert and insolent,
as though you were the injured person.

Jonathan Swift

When the strike of the hawk breaks the body of its prey
it is because of timing.

Sun Tzu

Surf or fight.

Colonel Kilgore

Never contend with a man who has nothing to lose.

Balthazar Gracian

Never interrupt your enemy when he is making a mistake.

Napoleon Bonaparte

An error is not a mistake until you refuse to correct it.

John F. Kennedy

When someone apologizes to you it is not considered politic
to interrupt.

Alice Liddel

Of the 36 alternatives, running away is best.

Chinese proverb

Exterminate! Exterminate!

The Daleks

First you expand the perimeter and then you lock down.

Naomi Klein

Honest disagreement is often a good sign of progress.

Mahatma Gandhi

People are afraid of dead air.

David Kipen

Whoever gossips to you will gossip about you.

Spanish Proverb

This calls for an aggressive marketing policy.

C. Montgomery Burns

Hope is a bomb, not a balm.

Tony Kushner

Conceit is the finest armor a man can wear.

Jerome K. Jerome

Do not weep. Do not wax indignant. Understand.

Baruch Spinoza

You make your decision and you live with it.

Alonzo Harris

Learn how to say, "I don't know". If used when appropriate,
it will be used often.

Donald Rumsfeld

One should never underestimate the capacity of the cynical
for sentimentality.

Matthew Parris

Dress like a bourgeois, think like a revolutionary.

Baudelaire

A good warrior will get out of the trench and march towards
the enemy even though he's terrified.

Marvin Gaye

Fighting's healthy.

Robert Evans

Confusion is mightier than the sword.

Abbie Hoffman

Destroy yourself physically and morally and insist all true brothers do likewise as an expression of unity.

Robert Hunter

There is no human problem which could not be solved if people would simply do as I advise.

Gore Vidal

Always forgive your enemies: nothing annoys them so much.

Oscar Wilde

" Words about Success "

You can make it if you try, all the way to the very top of the world (ma), and then there's nowhere to go but down, and success spoils even success...

A man who, after the age of 30, finds himself on a bus can count himself a failure in life.

Margaret Thatcher

The distance between insanity and genius is measured only by success.

James Bond

You have to be a bastard to make it, and that's a fact.

John Lennon

Success is never final. You have to take the glory in the pursuing rather than the capturing.

Herb Keller

It's all about ass. You kick it or you lick it.

General Groves

Show me a good loser and I'll show you a loser.

Paul Newman

If we don't succeed, we run the risk of failure.

Dan Quayle

There's what a man can do and what a man can't do.

Captain Jack Sparrow

The only place where success comes before work
is in the dictionary.

Vidal Sassoon

I always wanted to be somebody,
but I should have been more specific.

Lily Tomlin

Better to be a lion for a day than a sheep all your life.

Elizabeth Kenny

Fame's like having Alzheimer's disease.
You don't know anybody, they all know you.

Tony Curtis

I've been blamed for just about everything that's wrong with
this country.

Elvis Presley

Show me a hero and I'll write you a tragedy.

F. Scott Fitzgerald

The way you react to adversity is the key to success.

Tom Landry

You know the penalty for failure.

Ming the Merciless

Stardom is about who can twinkle.

James Coburn

A name made great is a name destroyed.

Hillel the Elder

Some are born great, some have greatness thrust upon them,
and some hire public relations writers.

Daniel Boorstein

The nice thing about being a celebrity is that
when you bore people, they think it's their fault.

Henry Kissinger

Celebrity is a pretty stunning thing.

Sharon Stone

Success is a great deodorant.

Elizabeth Taylor

Success didn't spoil me, I've always been insufferable.

Fran Lebowitz

Sometimes I'm so sweet even I can't stand it.

Julie Andrews

Success always occurs in private, and failure in full view.

Anon

Eighty percent of success is showing up.

Woody Allen

It's not enough that I should succeed – others should fail.

David Merrick

You have to learn to duck because they're gonna throw it at you.

Arthur Miller

Only those who dare to fail greatly can ever achieve greatly.

Robert F. Kennedy

Successes have many fathers, failures have none.

Philip Caldwell

I don't know the key to success, but the key to failure
is to try to please everyone.

Bill Cosby

Just when you think you've got the rat race licked – Boom!
Faster rats.

David Lee Roth

The thermometer of success is merely the jealousy
of the malcontents.

Salvador Dali

If you really want something in this life, you have to work hard
for it. Now quiet, they're about to announce the lottery numbers.

Homer Simpson

I have researched this, and the odds on winning the lottery
are the same if you play or don't play.

Fran Lebowitz

Try not to become a man of success,
but rather try to become a man of value.

Albert Einstein

When a man becomes preeminent he has to have enthusiasms.

Al Capone

The majority of men meet with failure because of their lack of persistence in creating new plans to take the place of those which fail.

Napoleon Hill

Success is that old ABC – ability, breaks, and courage.

Charles Luckman

If at first you don't succeed, failure may be your style.

Quentin Crisp

The only time you don't fail is the last time you try anything – and it works.

William Strong

Nothing recedes like success.

Walter Winchell

They never fail who die in a great cause.

Lord Byron

Sometimes I worry about being a success in a mediocre world.

Lily Tomlin

Fame was once seen as a recognition of your accomplishments
in the world. Now it just means being recognized.

Mick Hume

Things may come to those who wait,
but only things left by those who hustle.

Abraham Lincoln

Don't tell me how hard you work.
Tell me how much you get done.

James Ling

To infinity and beyond.

Buzz Lightyear

Thank you, thank you very much.

Elvis Presley

Words about Intoxication

A problem or no problem, stoned or sober, a natural inclination, or the embodiment of demons, pour another, score another, roll another, light up and let's talk about it...

Candy is dandy, but liquor is quicker.

Dorothy Parker

Why, oh why, didn't I take the blue pill?

Cypher

Why do I drink? So that I can write poetry.

Jim Morrison

The so-called virtues of sobriety are greatly overrated.

John Henry (Doc) Holliday

Wino forever!

Tattoo on Johnny Depp's upper arm

One martini is alright, two is two many, three is not enough.

James Thurber

Always do sober what you said you'd do drunk.
That will teach you to keep your mouth shut.

Ernest Hemingway

Dope will see you through times of no money better than money
will see you through times of no dope.

Phineas Freak

If smoking dope doesn't damage your brain, why do so many
Jamaicans believe a dead Ethiopian is God?

Darius James

Words are, of course, the most powerful drug used by mankind.

Rudyard Kipling

I never took hallucinogenic drugs because I never wanted my
consciousness expanded one unnecessary iota.

Fran Lebowitz

Electricity is actually made up of extremely tiny particles
called electrons, that you cannot see with the naked eye
unless you have been drinking.

Dave Barry

If you drink, don't drive. Don't even putt.

Dean Martin

When I read about the evils of drinking, I gave up reading.

Henny Youngman

Twelve steps can lead you to sobriety,
but one more will take you to the gallows.

Joe Gibson

An alcoholic is someone you don't like who drinks as much
as you do.

Dylan Thomas

Drinking makes such fools of people, and people are such fools
to begin with, that it's compounding a felony.

Robert Benchley

Reminds me of my safari in Africa. Somebody forgot the
corkscrew and for several days we had to live on nothing but
food and water.

W.C. Fields

To cease smoking is the easiest thing I ever did.
I ought to know, I've done it a thousand times.

Mark Twain

The trouble with jogging is that the ice falls out of your glass.

Martin Mull

The rest of the world is always one drink behind.

Dean Martin

I envy people who drink. At least they have something to blame everything on.

Oscar Levant

Turn on, tune in, drop out.

Timothy Leary

Cocaine is for horses, never for men.

Aleister Crowley

It's hard to be funny when you're coming off drugs.

Rodney Dangerfield

I only drink to steady my nerves.
Sometimes I'm so steady I don't move for months.

W.C. Fields

Whiskey has pushed more money across the table to sober players than all the bad luck and stupidity in the world.

Ned Buntline

Before you tell me that story again, let me take eight Vicodin.

Artie Lange

Avoid the green acid.

PA announcement

Relax. Have a cigarette.

Mr. White

Smoking kills.
If you're killed, you've lost a very important part of your life.

Brooke Shields

You know, it's cigarettes that killed Jerry Garcia.

John Mellencamp

Boy, make the world your ashtray.

Pete O'Toole

I feel that any kind of psychotherapy is contraindicated
for addicts.

William S. Burroughs

I hate to advocate drugs, alcohol, violence or insanity to anyone,
but they've always worked for me.

Hunter S. Thompson

I drink to make other people interesting.

George Jean Nathan

Chemistry is applied theology.

Owsley Stanley III

When I was in England I experimented with marijuana a time or two. I didn't like it, I didn't inhale it, and never tried it again.

Bill Clinton

The only thing I thought might ever kill me off was clean living.

Iggy Pop

Alcohol makes women more attractive.

Mayor Quimby

One more drink and I'll be under the host.

Dorothy Parker

We want the finest wines available to humanity, we want them here and we want them now.

Withnail

What I don't like about office Christmas parties is looking for a job the next day.

Phyllis Diller

Work is the curse of the drinking classes.

Oscar Wilde

Always there will be the intoxication of power.

Inner Party Member O'Brien

There's something addicting about a secret.

J. Edgar Hoover

Demand full sensory deprivation and back-up drugs.

Edina Monsoon

Mm-hmm. All the time! It's called Mescaline....
It's the only way to fly.

Choi

Reality is for people who can't handle drugs.

Elizabeth Wurtzel

I never had trouble with drugs, only with cops.

Keith Richards

Drugs have nothing to do with the creation of music.
In fact, drugs are dumb and self-indulgent.
Kind of like sucking your thumb.

Courtney Love

Get me a Percocet and a gin.

Eli Wohrman

Don't let it run you crazy. You liable to get killed.

Son House

It's better to be functionally drunk than dysfunctionally sober.

Hunter S. Thompson

Grandmother is over eighty and still doesn't need glasses.
Drinks right out of the bottle.

Henny Youngman

When you were drunk, the world was still out there,
but at least it didn't have you by the throat.

Charles Bukowski

A typical guys' day out. You get drunk and insult Indians.

Artie Lange

There's always someone ready and willing to sell guns
to the Indians.

Victor Renquist

The road of excess leads to the palace of wisdom.

William Blake

Teetotalers wake up in the morning knowing that's the best they're going to feel all day.

Dean Martin

LSD melts your mind, not in your hand.

Various attributions

When you machine-gun a vending machine, it makes a serious noise.

Kevin Roberts

There is only one cure for a hangover, and that is to drink a bottle of very, very dry Champagne the next morning.

Dean Martin

Plop, plop, fizz, fizz, oh what a relief it is.

Speedy Alker Seltzer

Words concerning Art and Creativity

From caveman to astronaut, humanity has striven to create, to leave its mark, to solve the problem, to make posterity take notice...

Why does art hate me? I never did anything to art.

Homer Simpson

Art is what you can get away with.

Andy Warhol

Art is in the wallet of the beholder.

Kathy Lette

Art cares nothing about respectability.

Lady Wilde

Art is making something out of nothing and selling it.

Frank Zappa

Art is merely the refuge which the ingenious have invented, when they were supplied with food and women, to escape the tediousness of life.

Somerset Maugham

Art, like morality, consists of drawing the line somewhere.

G.K. Chesterton

Art is either plagiarism or revolution.

Paul Gauguin

We must never forget that art is not a form of propaganda; it is a form of truth.

John F. Kennedy

Against the ruin of the world there is only one defense, the creative act.

Kenneth Rexroth

Acting is a masochistic form of exhibitionism. It is not quite the occupation of an adult.

Sir Laurence Olivier

When writers crack up, when they really end up in the nut house, is when they can't do it any more.

Kurt Vonnegut

It beats working.

Robert Mitchum

By eleven o'clock it's hard to believe you're not God.

Sydney Pollack (on directing a movie)

With all due respect to the world's great drummers –
it ain't brain surgery.

Mickey Dolenz

Think of Elvis.

David Lynch

Rhythm is something you either have or you don't have,
but when you have it, you have it all over.

Elvis Presley

There is no abstract art. You must always start with something.
Afterwards you can remove all traces of reality.

Pablo Picasso

I took up the guitar because I had a big nose.

Pete Townshend

Formlessness and chaos lead to new forms.

Jerry Garcia

If it's too silly to be said, it can always be sung.

Voltaire

Just because you like my stuff doesn't mean I owe you anything.

Bob Dylan

You do like Liberace, don't you?

Annie Wilks

Anyone who would paint a sky green and pastures blue ought to be sterilized.

Adolf Hitler

Children of the night, what music they make.

Count Dracula

Regression into childhood is the defining characteristic of modern culture.

Stephen Pollard

Writing requires total hermitage.

Edna O'Brien

Art today is institutionalized narcissism, a conspiracy between creators and curators to make poor people feel stupid.

Stephen Bayley

The first prerogative of an artist in any medium
is to make a fool of himself.

Pauline Ka

There are painters who transform the sun to a yellow spot,
but there are others who, with the help of their art and their
intelligence, transform a yellow spot into the sun.

Pablo Picasso

When all else fails, claim it's either poetry or performance art.

Mick Farren

It's a nocturne. You know, Frederic f**king Chopin?

John Henry (Doc) Holliday

I've sold too many books to get good reviews anymore.
There's a lot of jealousy, because critics think they can write
a good novel or a best-seller and get frustrated when they
can't. I've learned to despise them.

John Grisham

Originality is nothing more than judicious plagiarism.

Voltaire

If it reads easy, that's because it's writ hard.

Ernest Hemingway

When I want a cock and bull story, I'll read Hemingway.

Judge Constance Harm

The important thing in acting is to be able to laugh and cry.
If I have to cry, I think of my sex life. If I have to laugh,
I think of my sex life.

Glenda Jackson

Mistakes are almost always of a sacred nature.
Never try to correct them.

Salvador Dali

You could have the best joke in the world;
it still may not come out right.

Rodney Dangerfield

Comedy is tragedy plus time.

Woody Allen

I think it's the duty of the comedian to find out where the line
is drawn and cross it deliberately.

George Carlin

If you want entertainment, you can get a couple of hookers
and an eightball.

Sean Penn

I passionately hate the idea of being with it. I think an artist
has always to be out of step with his time.

Orson Welles

Acting starts with the hair.

John Turturro

The art of reading is to skip judiciously.

P.G. Hamerton

C'mon, give the singer some.

Jim Morrison

What's talent but the ability to get away with something?

Tennessee Williams

Get some floozies to run over you a few times.
That's where poetry lives.

Roger Alan Wade

An actor's a guy who, if you ain't talking about him,
ain't listening.

Marlon Brando

Suffering brings out the showman in a person.

Richard Powers

The tango is the dance of nihilism.

Argentinian nihilist

Somebody's overacting here.

Penny Marshall

Egomania is the natural ingredient of talent.

Martin Amis

There is not one female comic who was beautiful as a little girl.

Joan Rivers

Are you sure this is funny?

Margaret Thatcher

No one should ever drive a hard bargain with an artist.

Ludwig van Beethoven

" Words about History "

History may be bunk, and it may be written by the victors, but, according to some, we should not ignore it, at pain of being forced to repeat it...

For four-fifths of our history, our planet
was populated by pond scum.

J.W. Schopf

History never looks like history when you are living through it.

John W. Gardner

History is the version of past events that people have decided
to agree upon.

Napoleon Bonaparte

Studying history helps you avoid past mistakes, but it can't stop
you making new ones.

A.J.P. Taylor

Some people make headlines while others make history.

Philip Elmer-DeWitt

History will be kind to me for I intend to write it.

Sir Winston Churchill

Indeed, history is nothing more than
a tableau of crimes and misfortunes.

Voltaire

History is a relentless master.
It has no present, only the past rushing into the future.
To try to hold fast is to be swept aside.

John F. Kennedy

History is the short trudge from Adam to atom.

Leonard Louis Levinson

History is an endless repetition of the wrong way of living.

Lawrence Durrell

A man's eyes should be torn out if he can only see the past.

Josef Stalin

History is more or less bunk.

Henry Ford

People are trapped in history and history is trapped in them.

James Baldwin

Those who cannot remember the past
are condemned to repeat it.

George Santayana

The further back you look,
the further forward you can see.

Winston Churchill

If you can remember anything about the sixties,
you weren't really there.

Paul Kantner

Humpty Dumpty – did he fall or was he pushed?

P.D. James

It's the same f**king day, man.

Janis Joplin

History repeats itself as farce.

Karl Marx

History is a vast early warning system.

Norman Cousins

We would like to live as we once lived,
but history will not permit it.

John F. Kennedy

He left a Corsair's name to other times, link'd with one virtue
and a thousand crimes.

Lord Byron

Remember this: the past draws blood.

Jim Carroll

War is principally a question of maps.

Simon Jenkins

Only the dead have seen the end of war.

Plato

The gunfight was a spiritual exercise.

William S. Burroughs

The only good Indian is a dead Indian.

General Henry Sheridan

Recent history of mankind is the record of a vast conspiracy
to impose one level of mechanical consciousness on mankind.

Allen Ginsberg

We become both the subject and object of history.

Len Bracken

The last five hundred years seemed to race by.

Tony Soprano

No one likes armed missionaries.

Robespierre

If time were space, history would be a spider web.

Terence McKenna

There is nothing new in the world except
the history you do not know.

Harry S. Truman

Words about Truth and Lies

Ready for it or not, when we go to court we swear to tell the truth, the whole truth, and nothing but the truth, although, in our daily lives, the lie, ranging in shades of grey from white to the deepest black, is often the more practical option...

Deny everything.

Lenny Bruce

The truth will set you free, but first it will piss you off.

Gloria Steinem

When you have eliminated the impossible, whatever remains, however improbable, must be the truth.

Sherlock Holmes

The great masses of the people will more easily fall victim to a great lie than a small one.

Adolf Hitler

The truth is out there.

Fox Mulder

The truth is never pure and rarely simple.

Oscar Wilde

You're not ready for the truth.

Colonel Jessup

The truth is a knife and cuts sharp.

Charles Manson

If the truth doesn't save us, what does that say about us?

Lois McMaster Bujold

Truth is for suckers, generally.

Charlie Sheen

Nothing is what it seems.

Jim Thompson

And after all, what is a lie? 'Tis but the truth in masquerade.

Lord Byron

Yes, I'm lying, but hear me out.

Overheard in Hollywood

Facts! Facts! Behind them lies the whole foundation
of deductive truth.

Inspector Clouseau

If my life wasn't funny, it would just be true.

Carrie Fisher

As scarce as truth is, the supply has always been in excess
of the demand.

Josh Billings

The object of the superior man is truth.

Confucius

No one is entitled to the truth.

E. Howard Hunt

A little inaccuracy save tons of explanations.

Saki

You shall know the truth, and the truth shall make you mad.

Aldous Huxley

It is error alone which needs the support of government.
Truth can stand by itself.

Thomas Jefferson

It is always the best policy to speak the truth,
unless, of course, you are an exceptionally good liar.

Jerome K. Jerome

A lie told often enough becomes truth.

Lenin

I was provided with additional input
that was radically different from the truth.
I assisted in furthering that version.

Colonel Oliver North

It is hard to believe that a man is telling the truth when you
know that you would lie if you were in his place.

H.L. Mencken

A lie goes around the world while the truth is still putting its
boots on.

Australian proverb

Rumor travels faster, but it don't stay put as long as truth.

Will Rogers

One must know how to color one's actions and be a great liar
and deceiver.

Machiavelli

If you stop telling lies about me, I'll stop telling the truth about you.

Adlai Stevenson

There is fiction in your truth, and truth in your fiction.

Computer message from Animatrix

The man who says honesty is the best policy
is not an honest man.

Bishop Usher

We learn from experience that not everything that is incredible
is untrue.

Cardinal de Reitz

When I use a word, it means just what I choose it to mean,
neither more nor less.

Humpty Dumpty

The easiest thing in the world is to tell the truth.
Then you don't have to remember what you said.

Robert Evans

Some circumstantial evidence is very strong, as when you find
a trout in the milk.

Henry David Thoreau

How dangerous it is to believe exiles.

Machiavelli

All great truths begin as blasphemies.

George Bernard Shaw

We don't need white opinions.

Miles Davis

The truth is silly putty.

Paul Krassner

When a thing is funny, search it carefully for hidden truth.

George Bernard Shaw

An exaggeration is a truth that has lost its temper.

Kahil Gibran

Nothing is true...everything is permitted.

Hassan i Sabbah

People aren't getting enough truth.

George W. Bush

I'll believe that when pigs eat my brother.

Marlon Brando

There are only two ways of telling the complete truth –
anonymously and posthumously.

Thomas Sowell

The opposite of a correct statement is a false statement.
But the opposite of a profound truth may well be another
profound truth.

Niels Bohr

No one has conclusively proven that information is false, so it
may yet turn out to be absolutely true.

Ari Fleischer

Convictions are more dangerous enemies of truth than lies.

Friedrich Nietzsche

Nothing is so firmly believed as that which we least know.

H.L. Menckenz

Unless a man has a good enough memory,
he should never venture to lie.

Michel de Montaigne

Men occasionally stumble over the truth, but most of them pick
themselves up and hurry off as if nothing had happened.

Winston Churchill

The truth isn't beautiful, but the hunger for it is.

Nadine Gordimer

How I persist in my journey toward truth is inevitably dependent upon how bored I become before completing it.

Richard Meltzer

Never admit a lie. Just keep repeating it.

Joseph Goebbels

" A Few Words on Manners and Etiquette "

May be old fashioned, but they still maybe maketh man and woman something...

Manners maketh man.

William of Wykeham

A gentleman is a man who is only rude when he intends to be.

Winston Churchill

If you cannot think of anything appropriate to say, you will restrict your remarks to the weather.

Mrs. Dashwood

Do not speak of repulsive matters at table.

Amy Vanderbilt

If you haven't got anything nice to say, say it now.

Old maxim

Cleanliness and order are not matters of instinct; they are matters of education, and, like most great things, you must cultivate a taste for them.

Benjamin Disraeli

Good manners will open doors that the best education cannot.

Clarence Thomas

Don't reserve your best behavior for special occasions. You can't have two sets of manners, two social codes – one for those you admire and want to impress, another for those whom you consider unimportant. You must be the same to all people.

Lillian Eichler Watson

Associate with well-mannered persons and your manners will improve. Run around with decent folk and your own decent instincts will be strengthened.

Stanley Walker

Rudeness is the weak man's imitation of strength.

Socrates

Style is knowing who you are, what you want to say and not giving a damn.

Gore Vidal

Do not smoke without asking permission or sit so near (as in a train) that the smoke might annoy.

Amy Vanderbilt

Want to stand out? Try modesty.

Cindy Rodriguez

If you find a streak of vulgarity in yourself, nurture it.

John Mortimer

Only ugly people need manners,
the pretty can get away with anything.

Evelyn Waugh

The English disguise emptiness with impudence.

John Whistler

This is no time to be making new enemies.

Voltaire

He who makes a beast of himself avoids the pain of being a man.

Dr. Johnson

We are born charming, fresh and spontaneous and must
be civilized before we are fit to participate in society.

Judith Martin (Miss Manners)

" Words on Food "

Eloquence over food can, at times, wax as poetic as over love or sex...

There is no light so perfect as that which shines from an open fridge at 2 a.m.

Nigel Slater

Your produce alone has been worth the trip.

Prot

Grilled chicken is good when you fry it.

Artie Lange

Let them eat cake.

Marie Antoinette

Cake or death?

Eddie Izzard

Leave the gun. Take the cannollis.

Clemenza

Food is an important part of a balanced diet.

Fran Lebowitz

Donuts, is there anything they can't do?

Homer Simpson

Hell is other people at breakfast.

Jean-Paul Sartre

12% of Coca-Cola consumed in the USA is drunk at breakfast.

Statistic

You can only eat so much, you know?

Elvis Presley

Fat never looked good on anybody but babies.

Helen Gurley Brown

My definition of man is "a cooking animal".

Samuel Johnson

I suggest it's about time you considered salads.

Tony Soprano

Health food may be good for the conscience
but Oreos taste a hell of a lot better.

Robert Redford

The recipe for a happy life is a good digestion and a
bad memory.

Ingrid Bergman

You have a loaf of bread under each arm
and you're crying because you don't have
any ham?

Old Neopolitan saying

Red meat is not bad for you.
Now blue-green meat,
that's bad for you.

Tommy Smothers

Try the veal.

Captain McCluskey

Skinny women are evil.

Mo'nique

Are you hungry, my darlings?

Morticia Addams

There'll be no butter in hell.

Amos Starkadder

I refuse to spend my life worrying about what I eat.

John Mortimer

A hero is some kind of dumb sandwich.

Oddball

Go thy way, eat thy bread with joy,
and drink thy wine with a merry heart;
for God now accepteth thy works.

Ecclesiastes 9:7

Our lives are not in the lap of the gods,
but in the lap of our cooks.

Lin Yutang

Talk of joy: there may be things better than beef
stew and baked potatoes and home-made bread –
there may be.

David Grayson

Eat, drink and be merry for tomorrow you may contract
a horrible skin disease.

Edmund Blackadder

If you don't want a rotten apple, don't go to the barrel,
go to the tree.

Officer James Malone

I only care about whether we can eat. It doesn't matter
who's in power. We've never gotten anything from anyone
in power.

Jeanne Bazard of Haiti

Move where the food is!

Sam Kinnison

There ain't no such thing as a free lunch.

Robert A. Heinlein

Send a salami to your boy in the Army.

Sign in Katz's Deli, New York

No matter how you slice it, it's still baloney.

Alfred Smith

Whenever I watch TV and see those poor starving kids
all over the world, I can't help but cry. I mean I'd love
to be skinny like that, but not with all those flies and
death and stuff.

Mariah Carey

We shall eat lamb in Paradise.

Rizooli the Magnificent

The chicken tastes the same everywhere.

Tom Dowd

Most turkeys taste better the day after;
my mother's tasted better the day before.

Rita Rudner

Where's the beef?

Clara Peller

Fisssssssh.

Gollum

Guns will make us powerful,
butter will only make us fat.

Herman Göring

Please, sir. I want some more.

Oliver Twist

Don't go into Mr. McGregor's garden: your father had an
accident there; he was put in a pie by Mrs. McGregor

Beatrix Potter

Gobble gobble.

Butterball

I like fish and chips, but I like steak and chips more.

Ringo Starr

A dinner that ends without cheese is like a beautiful woman
with only one eye.

Jean Anthelme Brillat-Savarin

Where do you get quails' eggs at this time of day?

Emmett Honeycutt

Words on Morality

As with so many other things, there would seem to be far more talk about morality than action or practice...

These are my principles and if you don't like them I have others.

Groucho Marx

I wouldn't turn out the way I did if I didn't have all the old-fashioned values to rebel against.

Madonna

I try to be a person of infinite goodness.

Brigitte Bardot

Everything I want is either illegal, immoral, or fattening.

Alexander Woollcott

No one gossips about other people's secret virtues.

Bertrand Russell

Don't, by your attitude and movements, exhibit your body,
especially if you have a physique which turns heads.

Vatican advice to teenagers

Everyone is dragged on by their favorite pleasure.

Virgil

If I'd observed all the rules, I'd never have got anywhere.

Marilyn Monroe

You never know what is enough
unless you know what is more than enough.

William Blake

A good time is right. Anything else is wrong.

Kitty Twist

The good people sleep better at night than the bad people.
Of course, bad people enjoy the waking hours much more.

Woody Allen

Do what thou wilt is the only law.

Aleister Crowley

Evil is easy.

Pascal

My problem lies in reconciling my gross habits
with my net income.

Errol Flynn

To know all is not to forgive all.
It is to despise everybody.

Quentin Crisp

In the history of the world, no one has ever washed a rented car.

Laurence Summers

The time has come for everyone to clean up his own backyard.

Little Junior Brown

It's only when the tide goes out
you see who's swimming naked.

Warren Buffet

Moral indignation is jealousy with a halo.

H.G. Wells

All sins are attempts to fill voids.

Simone Wei

A great power is a great responsibility.

Spiderman

The greatest minds are capable of the greatest vices as well as
of the greatest virtues.

Rene Descartes

Income tax returns are the most imaginative fiction being
written today.

Herman Wouk

Nothing is more hard to resist than that which gives us pleasure.
All other argument is prudery.

Catherine the Great

The secret to life is honesty and fair dealing.
If you can fake that, you've got it made.

Groucho Marx

Jealousy is all the fun you think they had.

Erica Jong

We are here on earth to do good for others.
What the others are here for, I don't know.

W.H. Auden

The true civilization is where every man gives to every other
every right that he claims for himself.

Robert Ingersoll

Daddy says dice are wicked.

Todd Flanders

When choosing between two evils,
I always take the one I've never tried before.

Mae West

My life has been one long descent into respectability.

Mandy Rice Davies

Scandal is gossip made tedious by morality.

Oscar Wilde

Conscience: the inner voice that warns us someone may be
looking.

H.L. Mencken

It's not the temptations you succumb to in life you regret,
but the ones you don't.

Somerset Maugham

The worst crime is faking it.

Kurt Cobain

When your conscience says law is immoral, don't follow it.

Jack Kevorkian

If morals make you dreary, depend on it, they are wrong.

Robert Louis Stevenson

Do unto others as they do unto you, only do it first.

Hunk Houghton

You can imagine my embarrassment when I killed the
wrong guy.

Joe Valachi

There is only one way to achieve happiness
on this celestial ball – and that is to have a clear
conscience or none at all.

Ogden Nash

Too much of anything, however sweet,
will always have the reverse effect.

Marshall McLuhan

Words about Pets and Other Animals

They say that a four-legged friend will never let you down, although no one seems too sure about friends with beaks and tentacles...

The more I see of men, the better I like dogs.

Mme. Roland

The cat could very well be man's best friend, but would never stoop to admitting it.

Doug Larsen

Never teach a pig to sing,
it wastes your time and annoys the pig.

Nikita Khrushchev

Dogs look up to you. Cats look down on you.
Pigs treat you as equal.

Winston Churchill

Cats ruined the experiment.

Whiskas commercial

The average domestic cat will spend 10,950 hours purring.

Statistic

When I play with my cat, who is not to say she is not playing with me?

Michel de Montaigne

A cat can look at a king.

Proverb

Curiosity killed the cat, but for a while I was a suspect.

Steven Wright

The way of the wolf ain't no dog's life.

Charles Manson

Never wrestle with a pig.
You both get dirty, but the pig enjoys it.

Mr. Simpson

Live in such a way that you would not be ashamed to sell your parrot to the town gossip.

Will Rogers

125

I'm going to open a petting zoo in Germany.

Billy Connolly

You become responsible forever for what you have tamed.

Antoine de Saint-Exupery

Monkeys are lucky. Lucky Monkeys.

Artie Lange

A lot of liberal chickens got eaten by wolves.

Neil Young

My favorite animal is steak.

Fran Lebowitz

Kill the wabbit!

Elmer Fudd

Follow the tortoise.

The Tortoise

I know that the human being and the fish can coexist.

George W. Bush

Goldfish do not eat sausages.

RSPCA (according to Monty Python)

I loathe the people who keep dogs. They are cowards
who haven't got the guts to bite people themselves.

August Strindberg

Yesterday I was a dog. Today I'm a dog.
Tomorrow I'll probably still be a dog. Sigh!
There's so little hope for advancement.

Snoopy

It's funny how dogs and cats know the inside of folks
better than other folks do, isn't it?

Eleanor H. Porter

Animals are such agreeable friends – they ask no questions,
they pass no criticisms.

George Eliot

Fish like cheese...some fish.

Ozzy Osbourne

I don't keep a dog and bark myself.

Various attributions

A boy can learn a lot from a dog: obedience, loyalty, and the
importance of turning around three times before lying down.

Robert Benchley

The capacity of human beings to bore one another seems
to be vastly greater than that of any other animal.

H.L. Mencken

I will go and see if there is a rat in the rat-trap,
we could make a coachman of him.

Cinderella

If you are a dog and your owner suggests that you wear a
sweater, suggest that he wear a tail.

Fran Lebowitz

The common error made with ducks is trying to raise them like
chickens.

Raising The Home Duck Flock

A sleeping cat is ever alert.

Fred Schwab

Cats are smarter than dogs; you can't get eight cats to pull a
sled through snow.

Jedd Valdez

All animals are equal, but some animals are more equal than
others.

George Orwell

Put the bunny back in the box.

Cameron Poe

It's not the size of the dog in the fight, but the size of the fight in the dog.

Old Texas saying

The average dog is a nicer person than the average person.

Andy Rooney

No animal should ever jump up on the dining-room furniture unless absolutely certain that he can hold his own in the conversation.

Fran Lebowitz

Cats regard people as warmblooded furniture.

Jacquelyn Mitchard

If a pit bull romances your leg, fake an orgasm.

Hut Landon

Words on Identity and Character

Who are you? Do they really want to know? How do you know what they think when they see you, and do you care?

I think therefore I am.

Rene Descartes

I yam what I yam.

Popeye the Sailorman

It is I.

Michael Jackson

I don't know who I am.

Charles Manson

I'm a fat crook from New Jersey.

Tony Soprano

It ain't what they call you, it's what you answer to.

Bill Clinton

There are two types of people in this world. Those who like
Neil Diamond, and those who don't like Neil Diamond.

Bob Wiley

If I am not me, then who the hell am I?

Douglas Quaid

If you're the most average, can you still be just average?

Peter Inshaw

Talk low, talk slow, and don't say much.

John Wayne

Bad enough to be Jane without it being followed by Green.

Jane Green

I know who I was when I got up this morning,
but I must have changed many times since then.

Alice In Wonderland

Nobody can be exactly like me.
Sometimes even I have trouble doing it.

Tallulah Bankhead

Always remember you are absolutely unique.
Just like everyone else.

Margaret Mead

We are what we pretend to be, so we must be careful what
we pretend to be.

Kurt Vonnegut

Grass grows, birds fly, waves pound the sand. I beat people up.

Muhammad Ali

You've got smart people and you've got dumb people.

Keanu Reeves

My dad was not only sprayed with Agent Orange while in
Vietnam, but I think he was abducted by aliens too.

Marilyn Manson

If we could see ourselves as others see us we would vanish
on the spot.

E.M. Cioran

The nice thing about egotists is that they don't talk about
other people.

Lucille S. Harper

Humility is no substitute for a good personality.

Jon Winokur

We probably wouldn't worry what other people thought of us
if we knew how seldom they do.

Olin Miller

He has all the virtues I dislike and none of the vices I admire.

Sir Winston Churchill

We are products of editing rather than authorship.

George Wade

Smarter than the average bear.

Yogi Bear

A bear of very little brain.

Winnie the Pooh

When you feel in your gut what you are and then
dynamically pursue it – don't back down and don't give up –
then you're going to mystify a lot of folks.

Bob Dylan

Some people are funny.

Christopher Walken

To be or not to be, it was being.

Joe Hunter (Funk Brother)

Oh, I've never been real.

Quentin Crisp

Stay in your own movie.

Ken Kesey

Think of us as ships departing a sinking rat.

Robert Benchley

Some are born to sweet delight,
some are born to endless night.

William Blake

An optimist is someone who tells you to cheer up when things
are going his way.

Anatole France

The world is divided into people who do things and people
who get the credit.

Dwight Morrow

Pity the meek, for they shall inherit the earth.

Don Marquis

The guy could squeeze a quarter until the eagle screams.

John Gotti

The individual has manifold shadows,
all of which resemble him and, from time to time,
have equal claim to be the man himself.

Søren Kierkegaard

Anyone who hates children and animals can't be all bad.

W.C. Fields

Anyone who drinks Dom Perignon '52 can't be all bad.

James Bond

If you don't have enemies, you don't have character.

Paul Newman

Just because you are a character
doesn't mean you have character.

Mr. Wolf

" Words on Power, Authority and Government "

The Big Boss Man, his system, its different guises, and maybe how to beat or join them...

Unthinking respect for authority is the greatest enemy of truth.

Albert Einstein

Somebody has to be the boss.

Elvis Costello

His men would follow him anywhere if only out of a morbid sense of curiosity.

Anonymous grunt

There have always been tyrants and murderers
and for a time they seem invincible but in the end,
they always fall.
Think of it, ALWAYS.

Mahatma Gandhi

Communism is Soviet power plus the electrification
of the whole country.

Lenin

Communism doesn't work because people like to own stuff.

Frank Zappa

Politicians are the same all over. They promise to build a bridge
even where there is no river.

Nikita Khrushchev

Today's public figures can no longer write their own speeches
or books, and there is some evidence that they can't read them
either.

Gore Vidal

Those who make peaceful revolution impossible
will make violent revolution inevitable.

John F. Kennedy

Take away the right to say "f*ck" and you take away the right
to say "F*ck the Government".

Lenny Bruce

Liberty can't exist without security and order.

U.S. Department of Justice

Democracy is an abuse of statistics.

Jorge Luis Borges

The revolution is a dictatorship of the exploited against the exploiters.

Fidel Castro

The first duty of a revolutionary is to get away with it.

Abbie Hoffman

A liberal is a man who leaves the room before the fight starts.

Dorothy Parker

The people can always be brought to do the bidding of the leader.

Herman Göring

Revolution is a trivial shift in the emphasis of suffering.

Tom Stoppard

When we want your opinion we'll beat it out of you.

Right-wing catchphrase

True terror is to wake up one morning and discover your high school class is running the country.

Kurt Vonnegut

Distrust all those in whom the urge to punish is strong.

Goethe

People who think they're superior are exceedingly annoying
to those of us who really are.

Ronald Firbank

Success in almost any field depends more on energy and drive
than it does on intelligence. This explains why we have so many
stupid leaders.

Sloan Wilson

Your peasant is at heart a coward and a fool.

Count Dracula

I go the way that Providence dictates with the assurance
of a sleepwalker.

Adolf Hitler

A government big enough to give you everything
is big enough to take everything you have.

Benjamin Franklin

Any American who is prepared to run for president should
automatically, by definition, be disqualified from ever doing so.

Gore Vidal

Vote early and vote often.

Al Capone

And while the law (of competition) may be sometimes hard
for the individual, it is best for the race, because it ensures
the survival of the fittest in every department.

Andrew Carnegie

Kings, ministers, aristocrats, the rich in general, kept the people
in poverty and subjection; they kept them as they kept dogs, to
fight and hunt for their service.

Joseph Conrad

Agents of the world's elite have long been engaged
in a war on the populace.

Jim Keith

42% of office workers have fantasized about killing their boss.

Statistic

The young are generally full of revolt,
and are often pretty revolting about it.

Mignon McLaughlin

We shall now proceed to construct the socialist order.

Lenin

Under capitalism, man exploits man;
under communism it's the other way round.

Old Czech joke

If your boss is getting you down look at him through the prongs
of a fork and imagine him in jail.

Ricky Gervais

I am not here to answer questions.
Have you forgotten who I am?

Colonel Rosa Klebs

Beware the person in an organization who has never made
a mistake.

Stewart Steven

We know the system doesn't work
because we're living in the ruins.

Chester Anderson

Democracy must be more than two wolves and a sheep
voting on what's for dinner.

James Bovard

This is no time for jokes. You must rid the world of this filth.

Annie Wilks

There ought to be limits to freedom.

George W. Bush

The dissenter is every human being at those moments
in his life when he resigns momentarily from the herd
and thinks for himself.

Archibald MacLeish

This country, with its institutions, belongs to the people
who inhabit it. Whenever they shall grow weary of the existing
government, they can exercise their constitutional right
of amending it, or exercise their revolutionary right to
overthrow it.

Abraham Lincoln

Do slaves with big fortunes then govern us?

Remy Chevalier

Negation of life has been suppressed by the slaves who govern.

Len Bracken

It's good to be hated by the right people.

Johnny Cash

Most people have a natural instinct to rebel.

Elvis Presley

Blind faith in your leaders, or in anything, will get you killed.

Bruce Springsteen

Statesmen have to choose between evils.

Henry Kissinger

Don't get mad. Don't get even.
Just get elected, then get even.

James Carville

The whole aim of practical politics is to keep the populace
alarmed (and hence clamorous to be led to safety) by menacing
it with an endless series of hobgoblins, all of them imaginary.

H.L. Mencken

One has to multiply thoughts to the point where there aren't
enough policemen to control them.

Stanislaw Lec

Anyone who conducts an argument by appealing to authority is
not using his intelligence. He is just using his memory.

Leonardo da Vinci

When governments fear the people there is liberty.
When the people fear the government there is tyranny.

Thomas Jefferson

The problem is, whoever you vote for,
the government always gets in.

Old Anarchist saying

If the past and the external world exist only in the mind,
and if the mind is controllable, what then?

George Orwell

Hurrah for anarchy!

George Engel

" Words on Media "

No one is ever very happy with the media, and the more
they get, the less happy they are. Maybe it's because one of
the functions of the media is to bring bad news...

The medium is the message.

Marshall McLuhan

Half of the American people have never read a newspaper.
Half never voted for President.
One hopes it is the same half.

Gore Vidal

People have to enjoy the show.

Jerry Springer

People like to have their picture took.

Weegee

Reporters thrive on the world's misfortune. For this reason they often take an indecent pleasure in events that dismay the rest of humanity.

Russell Baker

There was a time when the reader of an unexciting newspaper would remark, "How dull is the world today!". Nowadays he says, "What a dull newspaper!".

Daniel J. Boorstin

Journalism is popular, but it is popular mainly as fiction. Life is one world, and life seen in the newspapers is another.

G.K. Chesterton

News is history shot on the wing.

Gene Fowler

No news at 4:30 a.m. is good.

Lady Bird Johnson

The window to the world can be covered by a newspaper.

Stanislaw Lec

The function of the press in society is to inform, but its role in society is to make money.

A.J. Liebling

Surely the glory of journalism is its transience.

Malcolm Muggeridge

A reporter is always concerned with tomorrow.
There's nothing tangible of yesterday.
All I can say I've done is agitate the air ten
or fifteen minutes and then boom – it's gone.

Edward R. Murrow

The journalistic vision sharpens to the point of maximum impact
every event, every individual and social configuration; but the
honing is uniform.

George Steiner

It's not easy being cool on television.

Neil Young

We tell the public which way the cat is jumping.
The public will take care of the cat.

Arthur Hays Sulzberger

Would it really be worth living in a world without television?

Krusty the Klown

From new transmitters come the old stupidities.

Bertolt Brecht

You can never get all the facts from just one newspaper,
and unless you have all the facts you cannot make proper
judgements about what is going on.

Harry S. Truman

By giving us the opinions of the uneducated, [journalism] keeps
us in touch with the ignorance of the community.

Oscar Wilde

Television has returned us to the picture thinking
of primitive men.

Marshall McLuhan

Never believe anything until it has been officially denied.

Old newspaper maxim

Never believe in mirrors or newspapers.

Tom Stoppard

The news gives you 5% of what's going on
and even that's distorted.

Charles Manson

The new electronic interdependence recreates the world
in the image of a global village.

Marshall McLuhan

The pen is mightier than the sword,
though not if your opponent actually has one.

Various attributions

It's my job to protect you from reality.

Fox Network censor

Rage is the only quality which has kept me, or anybody I have
ever studied, writing columns for newspapers.

Jimmy Breslin

The intelligentsia love the people,
but hate what the people love.

Theodore Dalrymple

What the crowd requires is mediocrity of the highest order.

Auguste Preault

The more one pleases generally, the less one pleases profoundly.

Stendahl

Literacy is almost dead.

Marshall McLuhan

The channels switch but it's all TV.

Andy Warhol

Never turn down an opportunity to go on TV or have sex.

Gore Vidal

War is show business.

Conrad Brean

It's amazing that the amount of news
that happens in the world every day
always just exactly fits into the newspaper.

Jerry Seinfeld

Television enables you to be entertained in your home
by people you wouldn't have in your home.

David Frost

The radio doesn't like anyone but me listening to it.

Taylor Mead

Amass a vast media empire.

C. Montgomery Burns

Seeing a murder on television can help work off one's
antagonisms. And if you haven't any antagonisms, the
commercials will give you some.

Alfred Hitchcock

A satellite has no conscience.

Edward R Murrow

If there's anything unsettling to the stomach, it's watching actors on television talk about their personal lives.

Marlon Brando

Imagine what it would be like if TV actually were good.
It would be the end of everything we know.

Marvin Minksy

Television is for appearing on – not for looking at.

Noël Coward

Words about Technology and Progress

Humanity seems no more comfortable with its progress than it is with its media, but we all like something new...

Did you know that the first Matrix was designed to be a perfect human world, where none suffered; where everyone would be happy. It was a disaster.

Agent Smith

The robot is going to lose. Not by much.
But when the final score is tallied, flesh and blood is going to beat the damn monster.

Adam Smith

The most likely way for the world to be destroyed, most experts agree, is by accident. That's where we come in; we're computer professionals. We cause accidents.

Nathaniel Borenstein

Technological progress has merely provided us with more efficient means of going backwards.

Aldous Huxley

Progress was alright. Only it went on too long.

James Thurber

The moment something goes into production it is obsolescent.

Alan Clarke

If you're working on things that everyone accepts, you're not working on anything.

Professor Alan Snyder

Growth demands a temporary surrender of security.

Gail Sheehy

A computer lets you make more mistakes faster than any invention in human history – with the possible exceptions of handguns and tequila.

Mitch Ratliffe

Reasonable people adapt themselves to the world. Unreasonable people attempt to adapt the world to themselves. All progress, therefore, depends on unreasonable people.

George Bernard Shaw

The world is so fast that there are days when the person who
says it can't be done is interrupted by the person who is doing it.

Anon

When they discover the center of the universe, a lot of people
will be disappointed to discover that they are not it.

Bernard Bailey

I would suggest we put the unit back in operation
and allow it to fail.

HAL 9000

That's one small step for man, one giant leap for mankind.

Neil Armstrong (on the first moonwalk, July 20, 1969)

Progress lies not in enhancing what is,
but in advancing toward what will be.

Kahlil Gibran

The universe is full of magical things,
patiently waiting for our wits to grow sharper.

Eden Phillpotts

Civilization is the distance man has placed between himself
and his excreta.

Brian Aldiss

He who builds a better mousetrap these days runs into material
shortages, patent-infringement suits, work stoppages, collusive
bidding, discount discrimination – and taxes.

H.E. Martz

Unquestionably, there is progress. The average American now
pays out twice as much in taxes as he formerly got in wages.

H.L. Mencken

Interestingly, according to modern astronomers, space is finite.
This is a very comforting thought, particularly for people who
cannot remember where they left things.

Woody Allen

The world is very different now. For man holds in his mortal
hands the power to abolish all forms of human poverty, and all
forms of human life.

John F. Kennedy

To confine our attention to terrestrial matters
would be to limit the human spirit.

Stephen Hawking

The scientific theory I like best is that the rings of Saturn
are composed entirely of lost airline luggage.

Mark Russell

155

Only be afraid of standing still.

Chinese proverb

Spin only operates when the washing machine is working.

Michael Brown

Machines have less problems. I'd like to be a machine.

Andy Warhol

It can only be attributable to human error.

HAL 9000

I'm quite happy to wear cotton, but have no idea how it works.

Edmund Blackadder

Computers don't have Swiss bank accounts.

Mary Fisher

The computer is a moron.

Peter Drucker

The most popular computer password is "password".

The Times of London

We have reached the limit of what rectal probing can teach us.

Kang

Any smoothly functioning technology will have the appearance
of magic.

Arthur C. Clarke

A déjà vu is usually a glitch in the Matrix.
It happens when they change something.

Trinity

For a smart material to be able to send out a more
complex signal it needs to be nonlinear. If you hit a tuning
fork twice as hard it will ring twice as loud but still at the
same frequency. That's a linear response. If you hit a
person twice as hard they're unlikely just to shout twice
as loud. That property lets you learn more about the
person than the tuning fork.

Neil Gershenfeld

If I had thought about it, I wouldn't have done the experiment.
Spencer Silver, creator of the Post-It

Just because you have a computer
doesn't mean you can't be stupid.

Butthead

Sped up my XT; ran it on 220v! Works greO?_|

Anon

I do not fear computers. I fear lack of them.

Isaac Asimov

If the automobile had followed the same development cycle
as the computer, a Rolls-Royce would today cost $100, get one
million miles to the gallon, and explode once a year, killing
everyone inside.

Robert X. Cringely

If it keeps up, man will atrophy all his limbs
but the push-button finger.

Frank Lloyd Wright

Our Age of Anxiety is, in great part, the result of trying to do
today's jobs with yesterday's tools.

Marshall McLuhan

You cannot fight against future. Time is on our side.

Lord Gladstone

Open the pod bay door, please, HAL.

Dave Bowman

Quit whining and go get a damn screwdriver.
I don't have time for this.

Computer tech support handler

Metaphysical, Cryptic and Bizarre

Just because it makes no sense doesn't mean it's bad advice...

What is the answer?...In that case, what is the question?

Gertrude Stein

Better stay inside, at least until the squirrels stop melting.

Marge Simpson

Accept eating by dogs and eternal spinsterhood.

Bridget Jones

If you don't like what you're doing, you can always pick up your needle and move to another groove.

Timothy Leary

At last fortissimo!

Gustav Mahler (on observing Niagara Falls)

My god, it's full of stars.

Dave Bowman (on observing another dimension)

Life is like Sanskrit read to a pony.

Lou Reed

The sidewalks were on fire and the bears were on fire
and I put them out.

Dutch Schultz

The worlds revolve like ancient women.

T.S. Eliot

Beware the big green dragon that sits on your doorstep.

Bela Lugosi

Its head will not be cone-like.

Fred Norris

Universal peace is declared, and the foxes have a sincere interest
in prolonging the lives of the poultry.

George Eliot

You're a pair of running dog reactionary revisionists, long live
Mao Zedong.

Alexei Sayle

Pigeons on the grass alas.

Gertrude Stein

Woopsy-daisy.

Bill the Butcher

If it's December 1941 in Casablanca, what time is it in New York?

Rick Blaine

2 is not equal to 3, not even for large values of 2.

Grabel's Law

Before you let the sun in, mind it wipes its shoes.

Dylan Thomas

Buy Goo!

Manhattan graffiti

Where does it say that Humpty Dumpty was an egg?

Frank McCourt

Needs must when the devil vomits into your kettle.

Edmund Blackadder

Nothing is achieved with chimeras.

Ernest Renan

No human being, no matter how great,
or powerful, was ever so free as a fish.

John Ruskin

It's hard to bullshit the ocean. It's not listening.
You know what I mean?

David Crosby

The Mystic Knights of the Sea will now come to order.

Kingfish

Viddy well, my droogs.

Little Malcolm

I shut my eyes in order to see.

Paul Gauguin

There are four lights.

Captain Jean-Luc Picard

I've been on a calendar but never on time.

Marilyn Monroe

The only sure way of catching a train
is to miss the one before it.

G.K. Chesterton

The Niburian mind-set has poisoned planet Earth.

Barbara Hand Clow

Go to the center of the gravity pull and find your planet, you will.

Master Yoda

Keep a clear head and carry a lightbulb.

Bob Dylan

It's a mystery wrapped in a riddle inside an enigma.

David Ferrie (alleged JFK assassination conspirator)

You dropped your f**king oranges.

Christopher Montesanto

Your hand is staining my window.

Nurse Mildred Ratched

The green eye is opening and closing.

Ben Stern

It was just a clever piece of cheese in the mousetrap.

Marilyn Manson

Miami beach is where the neon goes to die.

Lenny Bruce

Shazam!

Captain Marvel

Rosebud.

Charles Foster Kane

Rosebud is a sled.

Lucy Van Pelt

White magic is poetry. Black magic is anything that works.

Victor Anderson

Snatch the pebble from my hand, Grasshopper.

Master Po

Where are the eagles and trumpets?

T.S. Eliot

The twentieth century's over and I'm still not packed.

Jacob Rabinowitz

Existentialism means no one can take a bath for you.

Delmore Schwartz

Cough, cough...

Marguerite Gautier

Top of the world, Ma!

Cody Jarrett

The shortest distance between two points
is how far they are apart.

New York City graffiti

Don't have a cow.

Bart Simpson

Have a cow.

Gertrude Stein

We're through the looking glass here, people.

Jim Garrison

The numbers on opposing sides of a standard die
(as in dice) add up to seven.

Fact

The planet drifts to random insect doom.

William S. Burroughs

Words of Warning

We have been told we can never be too rich or too thin.
Apparently we can also never be too careful.

We have met the enemy and he is us.

Pogo

Always remember you're not me.

Keith Richards

Let us beware of common sense, inspiration, and evidence.

Charles Baudelaire

Beware of structure freaks.

Chester Anderson

Don't crowd anyone without a first-class reason.

Wyatt Earp

There's no getting blood out of a turnip.

Captain Marryat

The whole country's in a state of chaos.

Sean O'Casey

Never purchase beauty products in a hardware store.

Miss Piggy

We are not the doctors, we are the disease.

Alexander Herzen

Be virtuous and you will be eccentric.

Mark Twain

If you have a hammer, everything begins to look like a nail.

Friedrich Nietzsche

Patriotism is the last refuge of the scoundrel.

Benjamin Franklin

Loose lips sink ships.

WWII propaganda slogan

Don't wave your hanky at me.

Tony Soprano

Your arse won't touch the landing strip.

Ozzy Osbourne

Whenever you hear a man speak of his love for his country,
it is a sign he expects to be paid for it.

H.L. Mencken

I beat him when he sneezes.

The Ugly Duchess

Crawl, worm.

Mistress Natalie

For they have sown the wind, and they shall reap the whirlwind.

Hosea 8:7

It is not the light breaking through,
but the darkness settling down.

Dr. Vance Havner

The dawn of knowledge is usually a false dawn.

Bernard de Voto

Churning water, for however long a time,
does not produce butter.

Buddhist saying

Life is what happens while you're being afraid.

Stretch

Our swords shall play the orators for us.

Christopher Marlowe

I am not from your country.

Eddie Izzard

I'm going to get drunk, so hurry up.

Jack Osbourne

The enemy may come individually or he may come in strength.

General Jack D. Ripper

What we have here is a failure to communicate.

Captain, Road Prison 36

They only come out at night.

Stephen King

Superstition brings bad luck.

Dr. Saul Gorn

Everyone is alone in this town.

Eli Wohrman

It's not easy bein' green.

Kermit the Frog

These same reptilians have been occupying the bodies of the main players in the conspiracy.

Uri Dowbenko

We don't necessarily discriminate.
We simply exclude certain types of people.

Colonel Gerald Wellman

With all due respect, I have my own problems.

Mariah Carey

Life is just a bowl of pits.

Rodney Dangerfield

Beware all enterprises that require new clothes.

Henry David Thoreau

Beware the lash of vice and follies of the age.

Mrs. Centlivre

You don't know what enough is
until you've had more than enough.

Billie Holliday

There is no magic pixie dust.

IBM TV commercial

They are drunken, but not with wine.

Isaiah 29:9

Don't question me!

Patsy Stone

Cruel men cry easily at the cinema.

Graham Greene

Self-pity is the enemy of generosity.

Alexander Chancellor

Who so ever inhales the stink can never forget it.

R.D. Mangles

If you give it your little finger, it will soon have your whole hand.

Sigmund Freud

I will make you shorter by the head.

Elizabeth I

I'm going to pull your head off because I don't like your head.

Jeff Wode

Since everything is in our heads, we had better not lose them.

Coco Chanel

Any time your head explodes, that's like a tricky situation.

Tom Arnold

Surface at once. The ship is sinking.

Marshall McLuhan

The basis of optimism is sheer terror.

Oscar Wilde

I don't necessarily agree with everything I say.

Marshall McLuhan

No matter how bad things look, they can always get worse.

Ernest Lehman

What begins in fear usually ends in folly.

Samuel Taylor Coleridge

You are woozy from malaria.

Howard Stern

Old age is no place for sissies.

Bette Davis

Ah, this is obviously some strange usage of the word "safe"
that I wasn't previously aware of.

Douglas Adams

You never miss the water until the well runs dry.

Classic blues line

When the well is dry, we know the worth of water.

Benjamin Franklin

You carry your own water.

Max Hoover

We must be increasingly on the alert to prevent them from
taking over other mineshaft space, in order to breed more
prodigiously than we do.

Dr. Strangelove

Peace is our profession.

Motto of Strategic Air Command

Your commie has no respect for human life, even his own.

General Jack D. Ripper

We've failed to paint it black.

Jake

Stop endangering yourself.

Nelson Munz

It's a dangerous business going out your door.

Bilbo Baggins

Hope stings infernal.

Larry Wallis

Never look as though you're trying.

Shane Watson

Resistance is futile.

The Borg

You people mean nothing to me.

Hank the Angry Drunken Dwarf

Whatever is begun in anger ends in shame.

Benjamin Franklin

Posterity is as likely to be wrong as anyone else.

Heywood Brown

Posterity is just around the corner.

George S. Kaufman

I will remember not the words of my enemies,
but the silence of my friends.

Martin Luther King, Jr.

The attitude of human being to human being is unbelievable.

Ronald Searle

Nothing is so bad it can't get worse.

Extension to Murphy's Law

You can only have so much stuff.

Kelly Osbourne

I would advise you to make the explanation you are about to
give extremely good.

Edmund Blackadder

The way to be a bore is to say everything.

Voltaire

There is only one inborn error, and that is the notion we were
born to be happy.

Schopenhauer

Only the mediocre are always at their best.

Jean Giradour

Anything can happen in life, especially nothing.

Michael Houellebecq

To be angry is to revenge the faults of others on ourselves.

Alexander Pope

Beauty is only skin deep,
but ugliness goes clear to the bone.

Dorothy Parker

A good listener is usually thinking of something else.

Kin Hubbard

Good taste pops up when imagination dies.

Frank McCourt

There are only three sins – causing pain, causing fear, and
causing anguish. The rest is window dressing.

Roger Caras

Darkness will spread...darkness that can be felt.

Exodus 10:21

Behold, I will corrupt your seed and spread dung upon
your faces.

Malachi 2:3

Our lives are frittered away by detail. Simplify, simplify.

Henry David Thoreau

The road goes on forever.

Bilbo Baggins

Believing in the innate good of human nature and in the
inevitable triumph of virtue is invariably the cheery precursor
to the victory of evil.

Kevin Myers

Happy is f**king overrated.

You've got to take the bitter with the sour.

Samuel Goldwyn

Never drink black coffee at lunch;
it will keep you awake all afternoon.

Jilly Cooper

We are the people our parents warned us about.

Jimmy Buffet

Not everyone who has a body will admit it.

Tuli Kupferberg

Many are called, but few are chosen.

Matthew 22:14

Defeat never comes to any man until he admits it.

Josephus Daniels

Don't compromise yourself. You are all you've got.

Janis Joplin

To keep your character intact you cannot stoop to filthy acts.
It makes it easier to stoop the next time.

Katharine Hepburn

He who slings mud generally loses ground.

Adlai Stevenson

If you're ashamed of being a wallflower,
imagine how the wall feels.

Jacob Churosh

Attention to health is life's greatest hindrance.

Plato

There's one thing you can guarantee in life –
a surplus of pain.

Nick Cave

Nothing ever works out the way you want it to be.

The Oracle

Death is on your heels, baby.

Spike the Vampire

The purpose of life is to end.

Agent Smith

No more cat and mouse.

Inspector Clouseau

Before Elvis there was nothing.

John Lennon

" Words of Encouragement "

Maybe it's not as bad as you imagine. The sun will come up tomorrow, and you can make it if you try...

You have nothing to fear but fear itself.

Franklin D. Roosevelt

Discover the power within yourself.

Fortune cookie

This is the time for individual achievement.

Al Capone

Every man's a king, every woman's a queen,
and nobody wears a crown.

Huey Long

For what do we live but to make sport of our neighbours?

Jane Austen

Malice is one of life's pleasures, which only saints eschew.

Polly Toynbee

Blessed are the bewildered because they won't notice the difference.

Billy Connolly

Even a stopped clock gives the right time twice a day.

Various attributions

The new thing always has to start little.

Neil Young

There's no need to make things happen. They happen anyway.

Marlon Brando

Everything is possible if you wish hard enough.

Peter Pan

If I am going to spend eternity visiting this moment and that, I'm grateful that so many of those moments are nice.

Kurt Vonnegut

I'm tired of all this nonsense about beauty being only skin-deep. That's deep enough. What do you want – an adorable pancreas?

Jean Kerr

If you don't learn to laugh at trouble, you won't have anything
to laugh at when you're old.

Edgar Watson Howe

The older you get, the older you want to be.

Keith Richards

The blazing evidence of immortality is our dissatisfaction with
any other solution.

Ralph Waldo Emerson

I was glad to learn the truth about envelope stuffing.

Sheila Heffington

Where everything is good, it must be good to know the worst.

Francis Herbert Bradley

Dreams are wishes.

Dr. Jennifer Melf

Don't carry a grudge. While you're carrying the grudge,
the other guy's out dancing.

Buddy Hacketti

Everywhere is walking distance if you have the time.

Steven Wright

Time wounds all heels.

Bill Loud

Here's to the pencil pushers. May they all die of lead poisoning.

Eddie Valiant

If a thing is worth doing, it's worth doing badly.

G.K. Chesterton

Have no fear of perfection – you'll never reach it.

Salvador Dali

Start every day off with a smile and get it over with.

W.C. Fields

There's never a first unless someone starts it.

Frank Thayer

To undertake is to achieve.

Emily Dickinson

Less is more.

Various attributions

I hate the sun but it's nice to know it's there.

Johnny Rotten

Simplicity of language is not only reputable,
but perhaps even sacred.

Kurt Vonnegut

Excess on occasion is exhilarating. It prevents moderation
from acquiring the deadening effect of habit.

Somerset Maugham

If you enjoy it, it's okay.

Andrew Loog Oldham

What's the point of breathing if you're not betting?

Dr. Banzai

Housework can't kill you, but why take a chance?

Phyllis Diller

Often you just have to rely on your intuition.

Bill Gates

You may be disappointed if you fail,
but you are doomed if you don't try.

Beverly Sills

Hurry up and confess. Get it over with.

Carmella Soprano

And when man faces destiny, destiny ends
and man comes into his own.

André Malraux

People are valued more for what they endure
than for what they achieve.

Mick Hume

You've got a tiger; so unchain it and see what explanations
they give.

John Ashbery

Enchanting, but I don't think so.

*Peter O'Toole (on being offered the Academy Award
for lifetime achievement)*

There are worse things in life than death. Have you ever spent
an evening with an insurance salesman?

Woody Allen

Is there another way of looking at it?

Melvin Udall

Finally an end to the madness.

Lisa Simpson

" Words of Complaint "

One of humanity's greatest complaints is about how people complain...

I don't get no respect.

Rodney Dangerfield

Life is endless suffering.

The elder Zelig

Our peerless leader has flipped out.

Henry Kissinger

It's pathetic we're so easily manipulated.

Bill Maher

Who wants to see the Prince of Darkness crying?

Artie Lange

The world is so dreadfully managed,
one hardly knows to whom to complain.

Ronald Firbank

What a fine comedy this world would be if one did not play a
part in it.

Diderot

When we do good, no one remembers.
When we do bad, no one forgets.

The Hell's Angels Motorcycle Club

Who's got time to keep up with the times?

Bob Dylan

I coulda been a contender, Charlie.

Terry Malloy

There's not enough kindness in the world.

Dexter Gordon

What a revoltin' development this is.

Chester A. Riley

But a tawdry cheapness shall outlast our days.

Ezra Pound

He slimed me!

Peter Venkman

You loomed.

Dr. Jennifer Melfi

I want to be alone.

Greta Garbo

Make it all go away.

Jayne County

Hell is other people.

Jean-Paul Sartre

There's so many persons outside you can't deal with them all.

Bob Dylan

You're always outnumbered and you're always outgunned.

Socrates Fortlow

We are not amused.

Queen Victoria

I need someone to protect me from my enemies.

Henry Kissinger

Somebody has to do something, and it's just incredibly pathetic that it has to be us.

Jerry Garcia

The sublime and the ridiculous are often so nearly related that it is difficult to class them separately.

Tom Paine

The last time I was in a woman
I was visiting the Statue of Liberty.

Woody Allen

It should be, but it isn't.

Homer Simpson

The only normal people are the ones you don't know very well.

Joe Ancis

It must all be done over, everything that is must be destroyed.

William Carlos Williams

It's all so beastly.

Graham Norton

I'd hate to take a bite out of you. You're a cookie full of arsenic.

J.J. Hunsecker

But you did, Blanch.

Baby Jane Hudson

I'm not going to have some reporters pawing through our papers. We are the President.

Hillary Clinton

The people who know the least know it the loudest.

Ernst Anderson

People ask for criticism,
but they only want praise.

Somerset Maugham

Criticism is prejudice made plausible.

H.L. Mencken

People can be so damned selfish.

Mariah Carey

The only thing worse than having to give gratitude
is constantly having to receive it.

William Faulkner

You're making Happy Hour bitterly ironic.

Moe Szyslack

If I wanted to blow smoke up my own ass, I'd be home with
a pack of cigarettes and a short length of hose.

Don Brodka

Moses dragged us through the desert to the one place in the
Middle East where there is no oil.

Golda Meir

Some mornings it just doesn't seem worth it to gnaw through
the leather straps.

Mitchell Rothberg

I personally think we developed language out of our deep need
to complain.

Lily Tomlin

You're ruining my show. Goodbye!

Howard Stern

Words on Crime, Law and Justice

Crime doesn't pay because it is brought to justice by the long arm of the law. And if you believe that, we have some swamp land to sell you...

Behind every great fortune there's a crime.

Various attributions

The successful criminal brain is always superior.

Dr. No

Bad guys have the best clothes, cars, and dying scenes.

Eric Roberts

Banish wisdom, discard knowledge, and gangsters will stop.

Chuang-tzu

The day is for honest men, the night for thieves.

Euripides

Honesty pays, but it doesn't seem to pay enough to suit some people.

F.M. Hubbard

Honesty is the best policy – when there is money in it.

Mark Twain

The question is do you feel lucky?
Well do you, punk?

Harry Callaghan

If you ever see me getting beaten by the police, put down the video camera and come help me.

Bobcat Goldthwait

It was worse than a crime; it was a mistake.

Talleyrand

A liberal is a conservative who's been to prison.

Tom Wolfe

Let justice be done though the heavens fall.

William Watson

Those to whom evil is done do evil in return.

W.H. Auden

Wherein do the evil dwell?

Book of Job

The degree of civilization in a society can be judged
by observing its prisoners.

Fyodor Dostoyevsky

Prisons are built with the stones of law,
brothels with the bricks of religion.

William Blake

It was self-defense.

Liberty Vallance

I'm just a patsy.

Lee Harvey Oswald

Round up the usual suspects.

Captain Louis Renault

If you ask someone in the jailhouse for a story,
you get a jailhouse story.

Meyer Lansky

This business is filled with unrealistic motherf**kers.

Marcelus Wallace

Don't steal. The government hates competition.

Anon

It is no secret that organized crime in America takes in over forty billion dollars a year. This is quite a profitable sum, especially when one considers that the Mafia spends very little on office supplies.

Woody Allen

Once in the racket you're always in it.

Al Capone

A thief believes everybody steals.

E.W. Howe

We should go where the facts lead us.

Henry Kissinger

A policeman's lot is not a happy one.

W.S. Gilbert

Some men rob you with a six-gun, some with a fountain pen.

Woody Guthrie

Ever felt you've been ripped off?

John Lydon

Everyone has his reasons.

Jean Renoir

I gave birth to the 20th century.

Jack the Ripper

Scandal begins when the police put a stop to it.

Karl Kraus

If I learned one thing in the penitentiary,
you don't tell nobody nothing.

Charles Manson

The illegal we can do today; the unconstitutional may take a
little longer.

Henry Kissinger

If I can't see it, it isn't illegal.

Homer Simpson

It's not what you know, it's what you can prove.

Alonzo Harris

The United States is a nation of laws:
badly written and randomly enforced.

Frank Zappa

Honesty is the best policy, but insanity is a better defense.

Steve Landesberg

We are all guilty of everything.

Herbert Huncke

One should brave the underworld alone.

Edgar Allan Poe

Don't be a two-time loser, the penalty could be severe.

J.J. Hunsecker

These days it is better to appear guilty than impotent.

Tom Clancey

Get out of the way of Justice. She is blind.

Stanislaw Lec

Justice must not only be done, it must be seen to be believed.

J.B. Morton

You'll get nothing and like it.

Judge Smails

Never make a defence or an apology before you are accused.

King Charles I

If you want justice go to a whorehouse; if you want to get f**ked go to court.

Martin Vale

And God said, "Let there be Satan, so people don't blame everything on me. And let there be lawyers, so people don't blame everything on Satan."

George Burns

If it doesn't fit, you must acquit.

Johnnie L. Cochran, Jr.

I think capital punishment works great.
Every killer you kill never kills again.

Bill Maher

If guns are illegal only criminals have guns.

Bumper sticker

They'll take my gun when they pry it from my cold dead fingers.

Bumper sticker

Beware evil-doers, wherever you are.

The Masked Avenger

Words about Stupidity

One theory is that the stupid are really only there to make the rest of us look smarter than we really are...

Only two things are infinite, the universe and human stupidity, and I'm not sure about the former.

Albert Einstein

There are more fools in the world than there are people.

Heinrich Heine

Fools rush in where fools have been before.

Unknown

Man has never refrained from any folly of which he was capable.

Bertrand Russell

Fifty percent of the country doesn't know what 50% is.

Patricia Hewitt

Let us be thankful for the fools, for without them the rest of us could not succeed.

Mark Twain

Never underestimate the power of very stupid people in large numbers.

John Kenneth Galbraith

Stupidity is not the monopoly of the stupid.

Kevin Myers

It is to be remarked that a good many people are born curiously unfitted for the fate waiting them on this earth.

Joseph Conrad

Woolly thinking is for sheep.

Ben Elton

Traditionally, most of Australia's imports come from overseas.

Keppel Enderbery

It is dangerous to be sincere unless you are also stupid.

George Bernard Shaw

The problem of the global village is all the global village idiots.

P. Ginsparg

There's optimism and stupidity. It's a fine line.

Monty Livingstone

Egotism is the anesthetic that dulls the pain of stupidity.

Frank Leahy

To avoid abject stupidity a man must always be a little mad.

Michel de Montaigne

Una testa de cazi is Latin for "dickhead".

Fact

The hemp used in this garment is non-toxic and cannot be used as a drug.

Warning label

A great many people think they are thinking,
when they are merely rearranging their prejudices.

William James

People are proud of themselves for all kinds of dumb reasons.

Andy Rooney

Never attribute to malice what can adequately be explained
by stupidity.

Nick Diamos

You're so superficial it's disgusting.

Kelly Osbourne

Superficial is a good thing, right?

Jack Osbourne

If your eyes hurt after you drink coffee, you have to take the spoon out of the cup.

Norm Crosby

Artificial Intelligence is no match for natural stupidity.

Unknown

The two most common elements in the universe are Hydrogen and stupidity.

Harlan Ellison

Exterminate all rational thought.

William S. Burroughs

Rogues are preferable to fools as rogues occasionally take the day off.

Alexander Dumas

THIMK

1950s novelty sign

Everyone is entitled to be stupid, but some abuse the privilege.

Various attributions

To succeed in the world it is not enough to be stupid,
you must also be well-mannered.

Voltaire

Genius may have its limitations,
but stupidity is not thus handicapped.

Elbert Hubbard

Get all the fools on your side
and you can be elected to anything.

Frank Dane

To be stupid, selfish and have good health are three
requirements for happiness, though if stupidity is lacking
all is lost.

Gustave Flaubert

Ordinarily he was insane, but he had lucid moments when
he was merely stupid.

Heinrich Heine

There is nothing more frightful than ignorance in action.

Johann von Goethe

Half the world is composed of idiots, the other half of people clever enough to take indecent advantage of them.

Walter Kerr

Nothing in the world is more dangerous than sincere ignorance and conscientious stupidity.

Martin Luther King, Jr.

Men are born ignorant, not stupid.
They are made stupid by education.

Bertrand Russell

Everything that can be invented has been invented.

Charles H. Duell (in 1899)

Half this game is ninety percent mental.

Danny Ozark, manager of Philadelphia Phillies

Don't be stupid, you moron.

Ben Stern

You go to college to get stupid?

Sonny Corleone

Words about
Mental Health

In more primitive cultures the mad are treated with respect and even venerated, but civilization would seem to have cured us of that...

The definition of insanity is doing the same thing over and over again and expecting different results.

Oscar Wilde

Health consists of having the same diseases as one's neighbors.

Quentin Crisp

Every man has inside himself a parasitic being who is not acting to his advantage.

William S. Burroughs

It is no measure of health to be adjusted to a sick society.

Krishnamurti

Sanity calms, but madness is more interesting.

John Russell

Every normal man must be tempted at times to spit on his hands, hoist the black flag, and begin slitting throats.

H.L. Mencken

I suggest a vacation.

Mr. Lies

The wheel's spinning but no hamster.

Jerry Seinfeld

Nelly, you're a disgrace to depression.

Melvin Udall

Try not to be one of those people who find a slight in every compliment.

Max Rothman

The lunatics have taken over the asylum.

Conflicting attributions

When God closes a door, he opens a window.
My job is to not jump out of it.

Sharon Stone

206

The mad are all in God's keeping.

Rudyard Kipling

You're no crazier than some of the assholes walking the street.

Randall P. McMurphy

I was the kid next door's imaginary friend.

Emo Phillips

Having been dropped on my head as a baby,
I believe it helps.

Robin Williams

The real dark night of the soul is always at three o'clock in the
morning.

F. Scott Fitzgerald

It is possible that a certain amount of brain damage is of
therapeutic value.

Dr. Paul Hoch

Neurosis is a secret you don't know you're keeping.

Kenneth Tynan

Ideas or the lack of them can cause disease.

Kurt Vonnegut

Our envy of others devours us most of all.

Alexander Solzhenitsyn

When you're outside, we'll discuss whatever your problem is.

Nurse Mildred Ratched

I became insane...with intervals of horrible sanity.

Edgar Allen Poe

You have one more chance to be real.

Bill Murray

Horror and moral terror are your friends.

Colonel Walter Kurtz

Hehehehehehheheh!

Tommy Udo

Irony is the hygiene of the mind.

Elizabeth Bibesco

Noble deeds and hot baths are the best cure for depression.

Dodie Smith

We have nothing to fear but sanity itself.

Mork (from Ork)

The child gives in to nightmare while the grown man fears
his fear.

Jim Morrison

Resentment is like drinking poison and waiting for the other
person to die.

Carrie Fisher

Once upon a time crazy meant something,
now everyone's crazy.

Charles Manson

All things may corrupt when minds are prone to evil.

Ovid

The most merciful thing in the world is the inability
of the human mind to correlate all its contents.

H.P. Lovecraft

In this day and age, if you're not a public freak people assume
you're a private one.

Kevin Spacey

I told my psychiatrist that everyone hates me. He said I was
being ridiculous – everyone hasn't met me yet.

Rodney Dangerfield

The closer you look, the more we recede. We can't be found.

Richard Gere

For some people this world ain't ever going to be right.

John Henry (Doc) Holliday

To know all is not to forgive all. It is to despise everyone.

Quentin Crisp

It destroys one's nerves to be amiable all day.

Benjamin Disraeli

Reality is the leading cause of stress among those in touch with it.

Lily Tomlin

Insane people are always sure that they are fine. It is only the sane people who are willing to admit that they are crazy.

Nora Ephron

We do not have to visit a madhouse to find disordered minds; our planet is the mental institution of the universe.

Johann von Goethe

Insanity – a perfectly rational adjustment to an insane world.

R.D. Lang

Boredom. The desire for desires.

Leo Tolstoy

There's a very fine line between a groove and a rut; a fine line between eccentrics and people who are just plain nuts.

Christine Lavin

Egotism – usually a case of mistaken nonentity.

Barbara Stanwyck

Take a couple of years off and learn to be a human being.

Sandra Bernhardt

A Freudian slip is when you say one thing and mean a mother.

Larry Gelbart

Burn the house down. Burn them all.

Ralph Wiggum's invisible leprechaun

People who are shocked easily need to be shocked more often.

Mae West

I read somewhere that 77 percent of all the mentally ill live in poverty. Actually I'm more intrigued by the 23 percent who are apparently doing quite well for themselves.

Jerry Garcia

The world is faster than the mind.

Belize

I want to stay as close to the edge as I can without going over.
Out on the edge you can see all kinds of things you can't see
from the center.

Kurt Vonnegut

Show me a sane man and I will cure him for you.

Carl Jung

You need a mirror to see yourself.

Dr. Phil

You're only as healthy as you feel.

Travis Bickell

Words about Religion

If one fact is immediately clear, religion can mean all things to all people...

God does not play dice.

Albert Einstein

Atheism is the religion of the busy.

Fay Weldon

Can we skip church?

Homer Simpson

Dear God, I pray for patience and I want it now.

Short prayer

The happiness of heaven will be that pleasure and virtue will be perfectly consistent.

Dr. Johnson

God looks out for fools and drunks.

Various attributions

I will plague your whole country with frogs.

Exodus 8:2

Man is God's best friend.

Walter Bowart

Come down and redeem us from virtue,
Our Lady of Pain.

Algernon Charles Swinburne

Your attendant godling has lost her way.

Obscure fortune cookie

I don't believe in God, but I'm afraid of him.

Dean Keaton

No eye has seen, no ear has heard, no mind has conceived
what God has prepared for those who love him.

I Corinthians 2:91

Whenever I hear someone is in touch with God,
I look for the exit.

Arthur Miller

I never pray, it bags my nylons.

Jan Sterling

When I get down on my knees, it ain't for praying.

Big Nose Katy Elder

Play a nun? I'd rather eat glass.

Rita Moreno

Religion is the opium of the people.

Karl Marx

The true religion of America has always been America.

Norman Mailer

Sacred cows make the tastiest hamburger.

Abbie Hoffman

I'm a born-again atheist.

Gore Vidal

Chairs are an invention of Satan.

Lady Whiteadder

Praise the Lord and pass the ammunition.

Howell Forgy

215

The women were forced to wear hobnail boots to denote you as a penitent.

Mary Norris

In grief one turns either to the monastery or the brothel.

Roman Polanski

Saintliness is also a temptation.

Jean Anouilh

Know thee not that we shall judge angels?

St. Paul

Religion is the idol of the mob; it adores everything it does not understand.

Frederick the Great

I do not feel obliged to believe that the same God who has endowed us with sense, reason, and intellect has intended us to forgo their use.

Galileo Galilei

Cast aside those who liken godliness to whimsy and who try to combine their greed for wealth with their desire for a happy afterlife.

Kahlil Gibran

Question with boldness even the existence of a God;
because, if there be one, he must more approve of the
homage of reason than that of blind-folded fear.

Thomas Jefferson

I still say a church steeple with a lightening rod on top shows
a lack of confidence.

Doug McLeod

Everybody believes in something and everybody, by virtue
of the fact that they believe in something, uses that something
to support their own existence.

Frank Zappa

We have just enough religion to make us hate,
but not enough to make us love one another.

Jonathan Swift

He who doesn't dance can't reach god.

Sufi saying

Peculiar travel suggestions are dancing lessons from God.

Kurt Vonnegut

After the dance, the drums are heavy.

Haitian proverb

The devil is asleep or having trouble with his wife.

Ootah the Eskimo

Your karma is not mine.

Charles Manson

We must respect the other fellow's religion, but only
in the sense and to the extent that we respect his theory
that his wife is beautiful and his children smart.

H.L. Mencken

A long and wicked life followed by five minutes of perfect grace
gets you into Heaven. An equally long life of decent living and
good works followed by one outburst of taking the name of the
Lord in vain – then have a heart attack at that moment and be
damned for eternity. Is that the system?

Robert A. Heinlein

Do not envy a sinner; you don't know what disaster awaits him.

Old Testament

And all the men of the city shall stone him with stones.

Deuteronomy 21:20

A myth is a religion in which no one any longer believes.

James Feibleman

I won't take my religion from any man who never works except
with his mouth.

Carl Sandburg

I am determined that my children shall be brought up
in their father's religion, if they can find out what it is.

Charles Lamb

The opposite of the religious fanatic
is not the fanatical atheist
but the gentle cynic who cares not
whether there is a god or not.

Eric Hoffer

I'm completely in favor of the separation of Church and State.
My idea is that these two institutions screw us up enough on
their own, so both of them together is certain death.

George Carlin

Everyone ought to worship God according to his own
inclinations, and not to be constrained by force.

Flavius Josephus

For centuries, theologians have been explaining the unknowable
in terms of the-not-worth-knowing.

H.L. Mencken

Everybody likes to go their own way –
to choose their own time and manner
of devotion.

Jane Austen

The only shit in the Bible came out of
Pharoah's ass when Moses parted
the Red Sea.

Reverend Bertrand Sr.

Such evil deeds could religion prompt.

Lucretius

The true meaning of religion is thus not
simply morality, but morality touched
by emotion.

Matthew Arnold

The true mystery of the world is the visible,
not the invisible.

Oscar Wilde

The more I study religions the more I am
convinced that man never worshipped
anything but himself.

Sir Richard Francis Burton

All God's children are not beautiful.
Most of God's children are, in fact,
barely presentable.

Fran Lebowitz

With or without religion, you would have
good people doing good things and
evil people doing evil things.
But for good people to do evil things,
that takes religion.

Steven Weinberg

Say nothing of my religion.
It is known to God and myself alone.

Thomas Jefferson

And another of his disciples said unto him,
    Lord, suffer me first to go and bury my father.
But Jesus said unto him,
    Follow me; and let the dead bury their dead.

Matthew 8:21-22

To believe in God or in a guiding force
because someone tells you to is the height
of stupidity.

Sophy Burnham

Whatever God's dream about man may be,
it seems certain it cannot come true unless
man cooperates.

Stella Terrill Mann

It is an old habit with theologians to beat the
living with the bones of the dead.

Robert G. Ingersoll

If God did not exist, it would be necessary
to invent Him.

Voltaire

The greatest trick the Devil ever pulled was to
convince the world he didn't exist.

Verbal Kint

A cult is a religion with no political power.

Tom Wolfe

Words about Doing Nothing

Much is said about doing nothing, more, in fact, than one might expect...

It's good to do nothing and then rest.

Spanish proverb

Life isn't long enough for love and art.

Somerset Maugham

Hard work is damn near as overrated as monogamy.

Huey Long

Cover for me!

Homer Simpson

There are many ways of going forward,
but only one way of standing still.

Franklin D. Roosevelt

It was such a lovely day I thought it was a pity to get up.

Somerset Maugham

Work is the refuge of those who have nothing better to do.

Oscar Wilde

Never do today what you can put off till tomorrow.

William Brighty Rands

Life is something that happens when you can't get to sleep.

Fran Lebowitz

I wanted to be a singer because I didn't want to sweat.

Elvis Presley

I don't think necessity is the mother of invention –
invention, in my opinion, arises directly from idleness,
possibly also from laziness. To save oneself trouble.

Agatha Christie

Ambition is a poor excuse for not having sense enough
to be lazy.

Edgar Bergen

The art of being wise is the art of knowing what to overlook.

William James

It was like that when I got here.

Homer Simpson

Idleness is not doing nothing.
Idleness is being free to do anything.

Floyd Dell

Idleness and lack of occupation tend – nay are dragged –
towards evil.

Hippocrates

Laziness is nothing more than the habit of resting before you
get tired.

Jules Renard

Take rest; a field that has rested gives a bountiful crop.

Ovid

Indolence is a delightful but distressing state.

Mahatma Gandhi

Life is one long process of getting tired.

Samuel Butler

That indolent but agreeable condition of doing nothing.

Pliny the Younger

There is no pleasure in having nothing to do; the fun is in having lots to do and not doing it.

Mary Wilson Little

Far from idleness being the root of all evil,
it is rather the only true good.

Søren Kierkegaard

It's not work unless you would rather be doing something else.

J.M. Barrie

It's true that hard work never killed anyone but, I figure, why take the chance.

Ronald Reagan

The best way to fill time is to waste it.

Marguerite Duras

There is less to this than meets the eye.

Tallulah Bankhead

It takes character to withstand the rigors of indolence.

Lord Thurlow

Can't somebody else do it?

Homer Simpson

Nothing is as certain as that the vices of leisure are gotten rid of by being busy.

Seneca

The less one has to do the less time one finds to do it in.

Lord Chesterfield

I like work: it fascinates me. I can sit and look at it for hours.

Jerome K. Jerome

To spend too much time in studies is sloth.

Francis Bacon

It takes a lot of time to be a genius.
You have to sit around doing nothing,
really doing nothing.

Gertrude Stein

Genius only flourishes in the dark. Like celery.

Aldous Huxley

The greatest sin is to be unconscious.

Carl Jung

" Words about Life, Death and Fate "

As the end approaches...

If you die, you gotta be buried.

John Lee Hooker

I don't want to achieve immortality through my work.
I want to achieve it by not dying.

Woody Allen

You crawl out of your mother's womb, you crawl across open
country under fire, and drop into your grave.

Quentin Crisp

Your death will be peaceful and not at the hands of an assassin.

Mexican fortune telling card

Sometimes Mr. Mud kill; sometimes Mr. Mud not kill.

Mr. Mud

Once the game is over, the king and the pawn go back in the same box.

Italian proverb

Death is the only inescapable, unavoidable, sure thing.
We are sentenced to die the day we're born.

Gary Mark Gilmore

You hear that, Mr. Anderson? That is the sound of inevitability.
It is the sound...of your death.

Agent Smith

You gotta control the smiles and cries because they're all
you got.

Officer Jake Hoyt

Your food stamps will be stopped effective March 1992, because
we received notice that you passed away. May God bless you.
You may reapply if there is a change in your circumstances.

State Department of Social Services, Greenville, South Carolina

You can kill a man but you can't kill an idea.

Medgar Evers

A man who won't die for something is not fit to live.

Martin Luther King, Jr.

There is absolutely no inevitability as long as there
is a willingness to contemplate what is happening.

Marshall McLuhan

Good-bye. I am leaving because I am bored.

George Saunders (last words before suicide)

Death is peace from this world's madness.

Charles Manson

Death is nothing to us, since when we are, death has not come,
and when death has come, we are not.

Epicurus

Life is pleasant. Death is peaceful.
It's the transition that's troublesome.

Isaac Asimov

Any man's death diminishes me, because I am involved in
mankind; and therefore never send to know for whom the bell
tolls; it tolls for thee.

John Donne

For three days after death, hair and fingernails continue to grow
but phone calls taper off.

Johnny Carson

Never knock on Death's door: ring the bell and run away!
Death really hates that!

Dr. Mike Stratford

It's sad when our daddies die. Makes us one less person inside.

Pamela Ribon

On the plus side, death is one of the few things that can be done
just as easily lying down.

Woody Allen

What we have done for ourselves alone dies with us; what we
have done for others and the world remains and is immortal.

Albert Pike

One death is a tragedy. A million deaths is a statistic.

Josef Stalin

Many that live deserve death. And some die that deserve life.
Can you give it to them? Then be not too eager to deal out death
in the name of justice, fearing for your own safety. Even the wise
cannot see all ends.

J.R.R. Tolkien

All stories if continued long enough end in death.

Ernest Hemingway

I would not live forever, because we should not live forever, because if we were supposed to live forever, then we would live forever, but we cannot live forever, which is why I would not live forever.

Miss Alabama 1994

Today is a good day to die.

Klingon saying

If history had taught us anything it's that you can kill anyone.

Michael Corleone

Run over as many pedestrians as you can on the way to hell.

Marilyn Manson

Don't speed on the highway. The life you save might be mine.

James Dean

Don't threaten a man with a death wish. It only excites him.

Yancey Slide

Suicide is the sincerest form of self-criticism.

Anatole France

No matter what happens, there's always death.

Napoleon Bonaparte

Immortality, a fate worse than death.

Edgar A. Shoaff

Only rats, roaches, and Keith Richards will survive a nuclear war.

Richard Belzer

Why shave, when I can't think of a reason for living?

Jack Smith

Life is on the high wire. All the rest is waiting.

Bob Fosse

Tension is a killer.

Verbal Kint

If somebody has a bad heart, they can plug this jack in
at night as they go to bed and it will monitor their heart
throughout the night. And the next morning, when they
wake up dead, there'll be a record.

Mark S. Fowler

There's no cure for life.

Johnny Cash

The modern obsession with safety is killing us.

Alasdair Palmer

No politician is as popular as a dead one.

David Aaronovitch

Being born is like being kidnapped and sold into slavery.

Andy Warhol

Much further out than you thought and not waving
but drowning.

Stevie Smith

The evil that men do lives after them.
The good is oft interred with their bones.

Mark Anthony

The bad end unhappily, the good unluckily.

Tom Stoppard

We are in the speed up.

Marshall McLuhan

Our planet is on collision course with something we don't even
have a word for.

Terence McKenna

The future is not questionable.

Johnny Cash

If you want a picture of the future, imagine a boot stamping on a human face...forever.

George Orwell

Don't worry about the world coming to an end.
It's already tomorrow in Australia.

Charles Schulz

This is the way the world ends, not with a bang but a whimper.

T.S. Eliot

We move at high speed towards something none of us understands.

William Gibson

I have a feeling that when my ship comes in I'll be at the airport.

Charlie Brown

Quasimodo predicted all this.

Bobby Baccalla

It ain't over 'til it's over.

Yogi Berra

In all the taverns in all the world, she has to walk into mine.

Rick Blaine

We must believe in luck. For how else can we explain the
success of those we don't like.

Jean Cocteau

He runs into accidents which started out to happen
to someone else.

Don Marquis

I was a victim of a series of accidents, as are we all.

The Space Wanderer

Last night I stayed up late playing poker with Tarot cards.
I got a full house and four people died.

Steven Wright

I have always believed that all things depended upon Fortune,
and nothing upon ourselves.

George Gordon, Lord Byron

The end of the human race will be that it will eventually die
of civilization.

Ralph Waldo Emerson

Every man has his own destiny: the only imperative is to follow
it, to accept it, no matter where it leads him.

Henry Miller

Lots of folks confuse bad management with destiny.

Kin Hubbard

Fate is not an eagle, it creeps up like a rat.

Elizabeth Bowen

Doom on you.

The Tai-Kwon Dodoes

The tragedy of life is what dies inside a man while he lives.

Albert Einstein

Be sure he recalls his flimsy denials when he's face to face
with Death's sweet smiles.

Baron Harkonen

I am become Death: the destroyer of worlds.

Krishna

I am become Death, the destroyer of worlds.

J. Robert Oppenheimer (at the first test of the atomic bomb)

Kill a man and you are a murderer.
Kill millions and you are a conqueror.
Kill everyone and you are a god.

Jean Rostand

Crucial Observations

Among us are those who can see it more clearly, express it more succinctly, or both...

In two words, im possible.

Samuel Goldwyn

The dust of exploded beliefs may make a fine sunset.

Geoffrey Madan

A closed mouth catches less flies.

Irish saying

If you wait around long enough you'll get an answer.

Meyer Lansky

If I laugh at any mortal thing 'tis that I may not weep.

Lord Byron

There is false modesty but there is no false pride.

Jules Renard

There are 294 millionaires in Hampstead.

Statistic

Every man at three years old is half his height.

Leonardo da Vinci

It was a dark and stormy night.

Snoopy

How art thou fallen, O Lucifer, son of the morning!

Isaiah 14:12

In space, no one can hear you scream.

Slogan for the movie Alien

It's a small world, but I wouldn't want to paint it.

Steven Wright

Feel them out there, making their moves.

William S. Burroughs

One of the keys to happiness is a real bad memory.

Rita Mae Brown

There is something curiously boring about someone else's happiness.

Aldous Huxley

The pattern of human population growth in the 20th century was more bacterial than primate.

Edward O. Wilson

It's very depressing, people wearing overcoats in the house.

John Mortimer

Clothing is an extension of the skin.

Marshall McLuhan

Since global warming the Eskimos have 17 different words for water.

Euan Ferguson

It isn't pollution that's harming the environment.
It's the impurities in our air and water that are doing it.

Al Gore

We've got to pause and ask ourselves:
How much clean air do we need?

Lee Iacocca, President of General Motors

Everyone talks about the weather but nobody does anything.

Mark Twain

A world without string is chaos.

P. Schmutz

Save string.

The elder Zelig

Everything tries to be round.

Black Elk

Leaving the phone-booth I was struck by a whiff of the weird.

Jim Morrison

Travel is only glamorous in retrospect.

Paul Theroux

Good swimmers are the oftenest drowned.

Thomas Fuller

The ironing is delicious.

Bart Simpson

The word is irony.

Lisa Simpson

I've learnt from my mistakes and I'm sure I can repeat them.

Peter Cook

Next to a battle lost, the greatest misery is a battle gained.

Duke of Wellington

In the fight between you and the world, back the world.

Frank Zappa

We often make people pay dearly
for what we think we give them.

Countess Diane

There's nothing worse than doing the wrong thing well.

Peter Druker

We forgive those who bore us.
We cannot forgive those who find us boring.

La Rochefoucauld

To be a useful person always appeared to me to be something
quite horrible.

Charles Baudelaire

Gratitude is merely the secret hope of more favors.

Francois de La Rochefoucauld

You can't be around a comfortable person.
Nothing bounces off them.

Miles Davis

Nothing is more unpleasant than a virtuous person
with a mean mind.

Walter Bagehot

Adventure is nothing but a romantic name for trouble.

Louis L'Armour

An adventure is an inconvenience rightly considered.

G.K. Chesterton

A bore is a man who deprives you of solitude
without providing you with company.

Gian Vincenzo Gravina

Will a boy ever be born who can swim faster than a shark?

Gareth Keenan

There's nary an animal alive that can outrun a greased Scotsman.

Groundskeeper Willie

Learn to listen. Opportunity sometimes knocks very softly.

H. Jackson Brown Jr.

If you don't know where you're going,
you wind up somewhere else.

Yogi Berra

For lust of knowing what should not be known,
we take the Golden Road to Samarkand.

James Elroy Flecker

All that is gold does not glitter; not all those that wander
are lost.

J.R.R. Tolkien

The unfortunate thing about this world is that the good habits
are much easier to give up than the bad ones.

Somerset Maugham

There are only eight trustworthy people in the world.
There were twelve, but four were assassinated.

Danny Linquist

The world is quickly bored by the recital of misfortunes,
and willingly avoids the sight of distress.

Somerset Maugham

The bigger they come, the harder they fall.

Robert Fitzsimmons

The harder they come, the harder they fall.

Jimmy Cliff

The harder they come, the better.

Jenna Jameson

Tutti fruiti, good booty!

Little Richard

Gabba gabba hey!

The Ramones

Elvis has left the building.

PA announcement

Ha-ha!

Nelson Munz

" Words to Live by "

*From Cool Hand Luke to Jeff Spicolli – with Tallulah Bankhead,
Philip K. Dick and Mahatma Gandhi along the way – we now
bring you the A team, the best of the best advice...*

Sometimes nothing can be a real cool hand.

Lucas Jackson

The trick is never to get up before noon.

Charles Bukowski

Rome wasn't burned in a day.

Yancey Slide

If you don't see a sucker at the table, you're it.

Amarillo Slim (professional poker player)

Everyone's a mark.

William S. Burroughs

What, me worry?

Alfred E. Neuman

If eighty percent of the population poked themselves in the eye every Wednesday, would you?

Ozzy Osbourne

I want less corruption or more chance to participate in it.

Ashleigh Brilliant

The problem with people who have no vices is that generally you can be pretty sure they're going to have some pretty annoying virtues.

Elizabeth Taylor

Here's a rule I recommend: Never practice two vices at once.

Tallulah Bankhead

Don't try to solve serious matters in the middle of the night.

Philip K. Dick

The cynics are right nine times out of ten.

H.L. Mencken

Better to be a king for a night than a schmuck for a lifetime.

Rupert Pupkin

Smile. Tomorrow will be worse.

Woody Allen

Life sucks. Get a f**king helmet.

Dennis Leary

There will be no self-pity in the ranks.

William S. Burroughs

You must be the change you wish to see in the world.

Mahatma Gandhi

Whoever fights monsters should see to it that in the process he does not become a monster.

Friedrich Nietzsche

Do not meddle in the affairs of wizards, for they are subtle and quick to anger.

J.R.R. Tolkien

Treat all disasters as if they were trivialities
but never treat a triviality as if it were a disaster.

Quentin Crisp

If you are going through hell, keep going.

Winston Churchill

In skating over thin ice our safety is in our speed.

Ralph Waldo Emerson

A noble spirit embiggens the smallest man.

Jebadiah Springfield

Wide is the gate and broad is the road that leads to destruction.

Jesus of Nazareth

Make sure the knot in your tie is no bigger than a golf ball.

GQ

The fight does not always go to the strongest, nor the race
to the swiftest, but that's the way to bet.

Damon Runyon

Every child is an artist. The problem is how to remain an artist
once he grows up.

Pablo Picasso

Reality is nothing but a collective hunch.

Lily Tomlin

Reality is that which, when you stop believing in it, doesn't
go away.

Philip K. Dick

Reality is a concept with which to frighten children.

Coco Pekelis

We all started out as something else.

Lee Marvin

Keep a diary – and some day it'll keep you.

Mae West

A man should always know his limitations.

Inspector Harry Callahan

Cheer up. The worst is yet to come.

Philander Chase Johnson

Roll the dice.

Luke Reinhardt

Enjoy every sandwich.

Warren Zevon

It's the logical thing to do.

Lieutenant Commander Spock

Kill them all and let God sort it out.

Simon de Montforte

Absolutely goddamn right. Never get off the boat,
unless you're going all the way.

Captain Willard

When you find yourself trapped in a cage with a tiger,
you quickly learn in which direction to stroke its fur.

Chinese proverb

To live a creative life, we must lose our fear of being wrong.

Joseph Chilton Pearce

Make it gooder.

George W. Bush

If you're there before it's over, you're on time.

James Walker

Once the toothpaste is out of the tube, it's hard to get it back in!

H.R. Haldeman

The food tastes the same and you still get a year older each
birthday.

Richard Widmark

It is better to die on your feet than to live on your knees!

Emiliano Zapata

If you have to be in a soap opera try not to get the worst role.

Boy George

No problem is so large it cannot be run away from.

Charlie Brown

He travels the fastest who travels alone.

Rudyard Kipling

That which does not kill us makes us stronger.

Friedrich Nietzsche

There's always a Fredo.

Ian Speigelman

It's a campaign of fear and consumption.

Marilyn Manson

Beware the fury of a patient man.

John Dryden

Every pancake has two sides.

Gore Vidal's grandfather

Think sideways.

Edward de Bono

I always advise people never to give advice.

P.G. Wodehouse

Stay humble. Always answer the phone, no matter who else is in the car.

Jack Lemmon

Nothing goes out of fashion sooner than a long dress with a very low neck.

Coco Chanel

Do your damnedest in an ostentatious manner at all times.

General George Patton

One of the many lessons that one learns in prison is that things are what they are and will be what they will be.

Oscar Wilde

It takes a lickin' but it keeps on tickin'.

Timex TV commercial

A child of five could understand this. Fetch me a child of five.

Groucho Marx

Color is never quite as "in" as black.

Shane Watson

Passion is needed for any great work.

Che Guevara

The best victory is when the opponent surrenders of its own accord before there are any actual hostilities. It is best to win without fighting.

Sun-tzu

Half the time I make it up and it still turns out to be true.

Roy Cohn

Our capacity to perpetrate fraud now exceeds our ability to detect it.

Viktor Taransky

I laugh in the face of danger. Then I hide until it goes away.

Xander Harris

If you want to catch a fish, first learn to think like a fish.

Maori saying

If you stopped to think, you were lost.

Raymond Chandler

If a thing is worth doing, it is worth doing slowly ...
very slowly.

Gypsy Rose Lee

In games the object is to win, but in life the object is not to win. The object of the whole world is to preserve the game board and the pieces, and there is no such game.

Kurt Vonnegut

Hey, dude, let's party!

Jeff Spicolli

" Notes on Quotes

To say that collecting quotations is an art may be placing the
on the scale of human endeavours, but it is definitely a sport,
with big game hunting or fly fishing, although it excludes the
or wade in a freezing trout stream. The true collector reads bo
highlighter in hand, and watches TV armed with a pad and pe
have resorted to the tactic in the heat of a commercial deadline
already published collections is considered less than ethical an
admitted publically. The use of material from quote-of-the-day c
diaries is something of a grey area, permissible but not somethi
about. The best quotes are always the ones plucked from their

In a collection such as *Words of Wisdom* that ranges so widely a
philosophy, politics and pop-culture, the habitats are varied, exte
speeches of national leaders to dialogue from *Buffy The Vampire*
turn, spotlights the odd phenomenon that the remarks make just
and contain quite as much innate wisdom as the pronouncement

Mick Farren, 2004